ROUTLEDGE LIBRARY EDITIONS: LIBRARY AND INFORMATION SCIENCE

Volume 64

OPPORTUNITIES FOR REFERENCE SERVICES

OPPORTUNITIES FOR REFERENCE SERVICES
The Bright Side of Reference Services in the 1990's

Edited by
BILL KATZ

Routledge
Taylor & Francis Group
LONDON AND NEW YORK

First published in 1991 by The Haworth Press, Inc.

This edition first published in 2020
by Routledge
2 Park Square, Milton Park, Abingdon, Oxon OX14 4RN

and by Routledge
52 Vanderbilt Avenue, New York, NY 10017

Routledge is an imprint of the Taylor & Francis Group, an informa business

© 1991 The Haworth Press, Inc.

All rights reserved. No part of this book may be reprinted or reproduced or utilised in any form or by any electronic, mechanical, or other means, now known or hereafter invented, including photocopying and recording, or in any information storage or retrieval system, without permission in writing from the publishers.

Trademark notice: Product or corporate names may be trademarks or registered trademarks, and are used only for identification and explanation without intent to infringe.

British Library Cataloguing in Publication Data
A catalogue record for this book is available from the British Library

ISBN: 978-0-367-34616-4 (Set)
ISBN: 978-0-429-34352-0 (Set) (ebk)
ISBN: 978-0-367-37432-7 (Volume 64) (hbk)
ISBN: 978-0-367-37437-2 (Volume 64) (pbk)
ISBN: 978-0-429-35451-9 (Volume 64) (ebk)

Publisher's Note
The publisher has gone to great lengths to ensure the quality of this reprint but points out that some imperfections in the original copies may be apparent.

Disclaimer
The publisher has made every effort to trace copyright holders and would welcome correspondence from those they have been unable to trace.

Opportunities for Reference Services: The Bright Side of Reference Services in the 1990's

Edited by
Bill Katz

The Haworth Press
New York • London • Sydney

Opportunities for Reference Services: The Bright Side of Reference Services in the 1990's has also been published as *The Reference Librarian*, Number 33 1991.

© 1991 by The Haworth Press, Inc. All rights reserved. No part of this work may be reproduced or utilized in any form or by any means, electronic or mechanical, including photocopying, microfilm and recording, or by any information storage and retrieval system, without permission in writing from the publisher. Printed in the United States of America.

The Haworth Press, Inc., 10 Alice Street, Binghamton, NY 13904-1580
EUROSPAN/Haworth, 3 Henrietta Street, London WC2E 8LU England
ASTAM/Haworth, 162-168 Parramatta Road, Stanmore, Sydney, N.S.W. 2048 Australia

Library of Congress Cataloging-in-Publication Data

Opportunities for reference services : the bright side of reference services in the 1990's / edited by Bill Katz.
    p. cm.
"Has also been published as The Reference librarian, number 33, 1991" — T.p. verso.
ISBN 1-56024-137-3 (acid free paper)
    1. Reference services (Libraries) I. Katz, William A., 1924-
Z711.065 1991
025.5'2 — dc20
                                                                                   91-3285
                                                                                       CIP

Opportunities for Reference Services: The Bright Side of Reference Services in the 1990's

CONTENTS

Prologue: Ode to the Reference Librarian *Norman D. Stevens*	1

I. REFERENCE LIBRARIANS AT WORK

Joy Is Bustin' Out All Over *James Rettig*	9
Review of "Commitment"	11
Climate of the Late 1980s	12
New Guidelines Adopted in 1990	14
A New Vision for Services	15
Efforts to Limit the Vision	17
An Occasion for Joy!	19
The Fragile Allure of Reference *Paul Frantz*	23
The Archetypal Role	24
The Librarian as Counselor	26
The Relief of Randomness	27
The Reference Desk as "Catchall"	31
Reference Collegiality: One Library's Experience *Polly Frank* *Lee-Allison Levene* *Kathy Piehl*	35
Cooperation	37
Reasons for Change	39
Ready Reference Evaluation	40
Database Services	43

Bibliographic Instruction	45
Advanced Degrees	48
Conclusion	50

Technology and Service: Reference Librarians Have a Place in the '90s   51
    Mabel W. Shaw

Reference Librarians—A Critical Factor	52
Impact of Technology	54
Impact on Service	56
Conclusion	57

A Look Back at Twenty-Five Years Behind the Desk   59
    Constance A. Fairchild

University Reference Work	61
The Effects of the Computer	62
"Easy Rider" Comes to the Reference Desk	64
Conclusion	65

Librarians and Book Publication: Overcoming Barriers   67
    Mary M. Nofsinger
    Eileen E. Brady

Locating a Publisher	69
Locating Research Materials	72
Writing the Manuscript	72
Getting It Published	74

II. TOOLS OF THE PROFESSION

Ranking the Reference Books: Methodologies for Identifying "Key" Reference Sources   77
    Richard L. Hopkins

Definitive Answer	80
Generating a Basic List	83
Negative to the Positive	86

Making the Connection: The Telephone as a Creative
and Potent — but Underutilized — Instrument
for Reference Service   103
    Ken Kister

  An Ancient Technology   105
  True Stories   106
  Long Distance, Please   108

The Evolution of Early Visions: An Historical Perspective
on Today's Information Technology   111
    James Rice

  The Transformation of ADI   113
  The Impact of the New Professional Association   115
  One Big Library   116
  One Big Journal   118
  The Memex   121
  Conclusion   122

The Library of Congress Remote Online Library User
Pilot Project: The California State Library Experience   125
    Kathleen Low

  SCORPIO   127
  Multiple Use MARC System (MUMS)   130
  Search Structures   133
  Online Search Services   135
  Conclusion   137

HPER for Help: Selection and Reference Tools for a New
Field   143
    Elaine Cox Clever
    David P. Dillard

  Research Project Materials   145
  Guides and Lists   147

Legal Research Works for Non-Law Students   **151**
   Bill Bailey

   Joys of Legal Work   152
   Lighter Cases   154
   Spider Webs   156

Scholarly Communication, Peer Review, and Reference Librarian Ethics: A Case Study of the *Lexicon of the Middle Ages*   **159**
   Gordon Moran

   Peer Review   161
   A Case Study   162
   The Guido Riccio Controversy   163
   Stonewalling?   166
   "Computer Virus"   169
   Let My People Know   171

III. THE PUBLIC SERVED

The International Ideology of Library and Information Science: The Past Three Decades   **173**
   Stephen Karetzky

   The Equal Distribution of Information   175
   Cultural Relativism   176
   Conclusion   179

Strengthening the Foundation for Information Literacy in an Academic Library   **183**
   Laura A. Sullivan
   Nancy F. Campbell

   The Reference Environment   185
   The Technological Transition   187
   The Age Factor   188
   Conclusion   189

Community Cooperation in Reference Service via a Librarians' Liaison Committee *Margaret Hendley*	**191**
Impact on Academic Libraries	193
Volunteers and Reference Services with a Special Collection *Anne F. Roberts*	**207**

IV. POINTS OF DEBATE

Male Reference Librarians and the Gender Factor *Ronald Beaudrie* *Robert Grunfeld*	**211**

Prologue:
Ode to the Reference Librarian

Norman D. Stevens

SUMMARY. The reference librarian serves as the primary frontline professional responsible for aiding, either directly or indirectly, the library's users in their search for information. As such the reference librarian deserves our praise and commendation but such praise and commendation is seldom given in print nowadays as we tend, instead, to look at the downside of reference services be it burnout or the low percentage of reference questions that are answered correctly. Here, then, is an ode, although not in true poetic form, to the reference librarian that seeks to redress the balance by speaking of the noble feelings that we should all have for the essential professionals who serve Our Profession so well.

See the Reference Librarian and the joys that appertain to her;
Who shall estimate the contents and the area of the brain to her?
See the people seeking wisdom from the four winds ever blown to her,
For they know there is no knowledge known to mortals but is known to her;
See this flower of perfect knowledge, blooming like a lush geranium,
All converging rays of wisdom focussed just beneath her cranium;
She is stuffed with erudition as you'd stuff a leather cushion,
And her wisdom is her specialty—it's marketing her mission.

Norman D. Stevens is Director of University Libraries, University of Connecticut, Storrs, CT 06269 and is Director of The Molesworth Institute, 143 Hanks Hill Road, Storrs, CT 06268.

> How they throng *to* her, all empty, all grovelling in their insufficience;
> How they *come* from her o'erflooded by the sea of her omniscience!
> And they know she knows things, and her look is education;
> And to look at her is culture, and to know her is salvation.
>
> —Sam Walter Foss from *The Song of the Library Staff*

An *ODE* is a poem. It is also a means of expressing one's gratitude, in lofty sentiments, to a person for the services that they have rendered or the deeds that they have done. Sam Walter Foss' famous "Song of the Library Staff," for all of its overblown language and good natured jibes, is a true ode. It is, alas, one of the few pieces in our literature that sings the praises of the reference librarian. His comments on the reference librarian, noting in particular *her* accomplishments, are especially appropriate albeit somewhat out-of-date. My tribute to the contemporary reference librarian is, in a sense, a prose poem and is certainly intended to be an ode. Hail to thee!

I am *DELIGHTED* to have this opportunity to praise the work, and describe the traits, of the reference librarian who works in all kinds and in all types of libraries. He performs an essential service in facilitating access to our libraries by a wide variety of users. He does so both indirectly, by teaching others some of his skills in tracking down information, and directly, by tracking down that information himself in an increasingly complex information environment. In large libraries there is so much information that the user requires a skillful guide to what is there that matches her needs. In small libraries there may be so little information that the user requires an intelligent seeker who can lead her to resources beyond her own library. The user who knows a great deal about a subject needs an expert who can direct her beyond the bounds of her knowledge. The user who knows little about a subject needs a novice who can direct her to a simple starting place. The permutations of the user's needs is endless but, in every case, each need is important and is treated individually.

Foss spoke forcefully of the *ERUDITION* of the reference librarian of his time. Surely if that was true in 1906, it is even more so today. Our contemporary society relies increasingly on specialists who know certain aspects of a job, profession, subject, or task in great depth but who, too often, lack a broad knowledge of many subjects. Even within librarianship there are now numerous functional specialists who know only certain limited aspects of our work in detail. The reference librarian is not afforded that luxury. She cannot afford to be a specialist but must, in every circumstance, have a broad knowledge of the world, past and present, displaying, above all, an ability to deal with many questions, queries, subjects, and topics with equal aplomb, ease, and skill. Erudition is the key to excellent reference service.

The reference librarian is a *TEACHER*. In everything that he does he is not simply finding information but is teaching himself, his colleagues, and his users about the complex process of finding information. Each question, each search, each use of a reference work teaches the librarian something that he has not known and that he will be able to make use of in the future. Each contact and conversation with another reference librarian teaches her something new that he has learned that will help her in her work. Each action in helping a user to find a particular reference book or to answer a particular question teaches that user how to find that book or answer that question herself in the future. Each classroom lecture, orientation program, or seminar teaches a group of users a body of information that will guide them in their use of the reference collections and the library.

The *OWL*, for its association with, to the Greeks, Athena or, to the Romans, Minerva—the goddess of wisdom—has long been regarded as a symbol of wisdom. Athena or Minerva must be proclaimed the patron goddess of reference librarianship. Wisdom is, above all, the hallmark of the reference librarian. Pictures or statues of owls, as the universal symbol of reference librarianship, should be posted at or near every reference desk.

The user places great *TRUST* in the reference librarian placing in her capable hands his need for direction and guidance, and often for "the" answer, as he turns to the library as "the" place where his information needs can be met. She is much like Ann Landers, Dear Abby, Miss Manners, Emily Post, or other revered public figures to whom people may turn for personal assistance. The reference librarian is seen as an impartial authority in whose hand any question, even a barroom bet, can be placed with the assurance that truthful and unbiased information will be provided.

HONESTY is an essential, but often neglected, trait of the reference librarian. He must be able to know what he knows, and what he doesn't know, and be honest in explaining to each user the limitations of his knowledge. He must also be honest in his willingness to turn to other reference librarians, and other professionals, when their knowledge and skill may be superior to his and the key to providing a user with the right answer or the proper assistance.

A broad *EDUCATION* is needed by every reference librarian as she works with the user who, whether educated or uneducated, brings to his quest for assistance questions on many and varied subjects. The reference librarian knows just enough about many subjects, and a great deal about some, to be able to understand and interpret the user's question. Education is the key not only to knowing the reference collection and reference techniques but knowing the language of the field that a user is pursuing in order to be able to guide him to, and through, the right reference tools.

The reference librarian *READS* omnivorously. The excellent reference librarian heeds John Cotton Dana's classic twelve rules.

1. Read.
2. Read.
3. Read some more.
4. Read anything.
5. Read about everything.
6. Read enjoyable things.
7. Read things you yourself enjoy.
8. Read, and talk about it.
9. Read very carefully, some things.
10. Read on the run, most things.
11. Don't think about reading, but
12. Just read.

The *EYES* of the reference librarian are always alert to what is happening around him. He is ever watchful of the reactions of the individual user whom he may be assisting in order to understand whether or not that person is being aided or confused. He is also, even while helping one user, watchful of what is happening in the reference room so that he can assist others who may be in need of help but reluctant to ask for it.

When asked to describe the chief requirement of a reference librarian, one answer is good *FEET*. While some librarians, especially administrators, spend much of their time sitting at a desk, the active reference librarian, whose feet are an indicator of her stamina, uses the reference desk as her starting point. Reference books are not to be pointed at but are to be taken to; only by moving actively and quickly about the reference room, can proper instruction on the content and use of the collection be given.

The reference librarian uses his *EARS* to listen for the telephone and sometimes for a small bell that may summon him back to the reference desk when a user needs assistance. But above all the reference librarian uses his ears to listen carefully to the questions asked by the user. The knack of sorting out what a user already knows from what she does not know, or what she is really looking for from what she says she wants, is a trait inbred in the reference librarian. By listening carefully, with both ears, he is able to interpret questions, discern needs, determine appropriate sources, and guide the user quickly to the information that will answer her inquiry.

Yes John Cotton Dana was right! *READ*, read, and read some more. It is only by reading a wide variety of material, not simply new reference books or special subject treatises but contemporary and popular items, constantly that the reference librarian maintains a keen awareness of the world about her and the issues and topics that users will invariably ask about.

The *ENERGY* displayed by the reference librarian as he whirls about the department and the library pursuing information is truly amazing. Often a blur as he passes by, with a nod and a smile but seldom time for a hello, the reference librarian dances from question to question, user to user, and spot to spot with indefatigable enthusiasm spurred on only by his dedication to his work and perhaps an occasional candy bar.

The *NOISE* of the contemporary library, which can be especially intense in a busy reference room, is, in vital contrast to the silence that once prevailed in libraries, a splendid sign of the intense activity that is involved in aiding users. The reference librarian has a remarkable ability to concentrate on the task at hand and to exclude extraneous noise while at the same time selecting from the noise around her bits and snatches of relevant information. She is most adept at extracting from the noise a sense of when one of her colleagues or a user needs assistance or information that she can readily supply.

The reference librarian is always *COOL* in face of the intense pressure that he often faces when there are a number of users all with difficult questions anxiously but, hopefully, patiently waiting for his help. The intense pressure, the variety of questions that require rapid adaptation, the complexity or simplicity of the user's inquiry, his success or failure in finding the right answer in a timely fashion, and the complaints or compliments from the user seldom faze him. He takes it all good-naturedly in stride and moves calmly and quickly on to the next adventure.

Always *EFFICIENT* the reference librarian organizes her desk, her time, her work, and even—if she is truly efficient—her path through the reference room so as to make the best use of her time. Efficiency is an essential key to her ability to accomplish all of the normal duties that her job entails while simultaneously responding to the constant demands that arrive without warning and that often take priority over whatever else she may have been expecting to accomplish during that day or even at that moment.

The reference librarian displays *LEADERSHIP* in his department, his library, and his profession. He shows others the way especially by deed and example as he strives to meet the simple and complex challenges of contemporary librarianship. Through his leadership, the reference librarian establishes his credentials and the importance of reference work to the effective provision of the best possible service in a library.

INTELLIGENCE like wisdom is honored and respected by the reference librarian but, at the same time, she does not scorn ignorance. Intelligence is a virtue in the reference librarian for it gives her a broad grasp of the world of knowledge that enables her to better carry out her work. Intelligence is a virtue to the reference librarian for it gives her the opportunity to be challenged and stimulated by others and, in responding to those challenges and that stimulation, she expands her own information and intelligence still further.

The reference librarian is *BOLD* in responding to the challenges of librarianship and being at all times on the cutting edge of his profession. He readily learns new information, steps forward to accept new assignments, assimilates new information, responds with enthusiasm to a new user, and is eager to find new ways to improve his performance. No question is too hard. No subject is too arcane. No reference tool is too complex. No user is too trying. Everything is to be learned, mastered, and shared.

To engage in and support *RESEARCH* is what the reference librarian does best. Answering specific questions—even the location of the restroom—or offering bibliographic instruction—even to beginning students—are important tasks that the reference librarian generally undertakes willingly and with pleasure. Examining issues in depth whether simply for her own elucidation, for the purposes of acquiring newfound knowledge that can be shared with others, or in assistance to a user who may be writing a term paper or a scholarly essay are essential tasks that she always undertakes enthusiastically and with delight. The commitment, dedication, and persistence of the reference librarian is never more evident than when she is engaged in bringing together a body of ideas and information as she helps create knowledge.

The primary *ATTITUDE* of the reference librarian is inevitably caring, cheerful, and courteous. That attitude allows him to convey to each and every user a true sense of personal concern that transcends the particular encounter or the particular question. Through his positive attitude the reference librarian provides the user with a sense that her question is important, her satisfaction is paramount, and her business is welcome.

Ever *READY* to answer any question, and to accept any challenge, the reference librarian displays her eagerness to all who come before her. The user who approaches the reference desk knows that he will find her there ready, able, and willing to assist him. Her colleague in the department or in the library who wants assistance with a personal or a professional inquiry knows that he too will find that same ready spirit. Even the department head or administrator who asks her to serve on yet another committee will, usually, find her ready to take on even that assignment with a smile and a steady hand.

IGNORANCE is the sworn enemy of the reference librarian. He attacks it with persistence and vigor. He seeks to shed the light of information on the darkness of ignorance thus bringing knowledge to his user. Nothing troubles the reference librarian so much as the lack of information that a user has brought with her when she turns to him for help. Nothing pleases the reference librarian so much as the wealth of information which makes the user a much wiser person.

The reference librarian is ACTIVE not passive even when engaged in such a seemingly passive pursuit as reading. She reads to learn so that she can put that learning to active use. She is active in her daily work so that she can learn more about what is happening in the library and what library users are interested in. She is active in the broader work of her library so that she can help shape its services to better meet the reference needs of users. She is active in her profession so that she can learn of new developments and trends and find ways to apply what she has learned to the work of her library and her department.

The NOBLEST librarian of all is, without question, the reference librarian.

—"Atque in perpetuum, frater [et soror], ave atque vale!"

I. REFERENCE LIBRARIANS AT WORK

Joy Is Bustin' Out All Over

James Rettig

SUMMARY. When the American Library Association's Reference and Adult Services Division adopted "Information Services for Information Consumers: Guidelines for Providers" in June of 1990, it set the positive tone that reference work can and should have throughout the decade and beyond. Efforts by corporations to promote end-user online services, consumer-oriented CD-ROMs, and the like constitute an attempt to recreate the library. These attempts are, however, inherently flawed in that, unlike the library, they do not marshal the wide variety of information resources—print, online, CD-ROM, audio-visual, etc.—that libraries routinely make available. "Information Services for Information Consumers: Guidelines for Providers" challenges information providers (i.e., libraries and reference librarians) to take full advantage of new information and communications technology to make not only the services marketed to end users useful to library patrons, but to realize more fully the potential of the rich resources already concentrated in libraries. The guidelines offer reference librarians and library ad-

---

James Rettig is Assistant University Librarian for Reference and Information Services, Earl Gregg Swem Library, College of William and Mary, Williamsburg, VA 23187.

ministrators and governing boards a vision of a comprehensive information service centered in and delivered by the library to the members of the community it is intended to serve. They also challenge reference librarians, library administrators, and governing boards to make that vision a reality. This will require creativity, entail some risks, and depend for its success upon the quality of the resources allocated to the task. The most important variable will be the quality of the front-line reference librarians and their commitment to that vision and the spirit of the guidelines.

Introductory note: This article discusses in considerable detail the American Library Association's Reference and Adult Services Division's "Information Services for Information Consumers: Guidelines for Providers." The author chaired the RASD subcommittee that drafted this document. All opinions expressed in this article and all interpretations of the document itself are the author's personal views; they are not nor should they be considered statements of or on behalf of the ALA Reference and Adult Services Division.

The familiar song "June is Bustin' Out All Over" from Rogers and Hammerstein's *Carousel* celebrates the coming of summer, the spring-induced stirring of generativity experienced by all of nature, and the joy young people feel anticipating the delicious, delightful pleasures of summer. Several years ago, reference librarianship experienced what one commentator described as its "deep winter."[1] The sources of that discontent were analyzed in two much discussed articles, Charles Bunge's "Potential and Reality at the Reference Desk: Reflections on a 'Return to the Field,'" and William Miller's "What's Wrong with Reference."[2] In the mid-1980s, the field's most insightful critics found much cause for worry and little promise of joy. Reference librarians were struggling with the challenge of serving an ever increasingly diverse clientele, many of whose members had little experience of library services; the challenge of integrating new technologies into a traditionally low-tech, print-based service; and the challenge of staying fresh and sustaining enthusiasm while fielding the same frequently asked questions again and again and again.

In this climate the American Library Association's Reference and Adult Services Division chose to cast some warming rays of sunshine by revising its guidelines for reference services. The guidelines, published as "A Commitment to Information Services: Developmental Guidelines" had been adopted by RASD in 1976 and amended by the addition of a section on professional ethics in 1979.[3] The impetus for the review of this document was a request in January of 1985 by the RASD Evaluation of Reference and Adult Services Committee to revise the section dealing with evaluation of services. Rather than take a piecemeal approach to such an important statement of organizational philosophy, RASD chose in the next summer to appoint an ad hoc subcommittee of its Standards and Guidelines Committee to review the entire document and make recommendations for its revision. Bureaucratic delays, an ever present danger in ALA, meant that a subcommittee was not formed until late 1987 and was not able to begin work on its task until the spring of 1988.

REVIEW OF "COMMITMENT"

That work began, of course, with a review and critique of "A Commitment to Information Services." A call for comments from the field elicited little response. Left to its own devices, the subcommittee concluded that "Commitment" was a monumental document in that it was the first attempt to articulate standards for reference and information services. However, it was also, as any document inevitably is, a creature of its times, in this case the mid-1970s, a time when online access to remote databases had only recently begun to penetrate libraries and librarians debated whether this new service should be integrated with reference departments or ensconced in its own department physically separate from the reference department. Various statements in the document reveal, with the clarity only hindsight offers, the values of the time. For example, the statement "The reference or information collection should be situated so that it is near an open area where access allows for quick and effective service,"[4] rests on the supposition that information services are inextricably linked to on-site resources. And the

"Draft Outline of Information Service Policy Manual," an appendix to the guidelines, includes among its categories of service "Card catalog service,"[5] a service that is not yet an anachronism in the early 1990s, but in many libraries is well on its way to becoming one. The 1976 guidelines include hints that change is imminent; "electronic means" are mentioned in the document's one footnote and there is reference to "information data bases," a term the document does not define, either explicitly or implicitly through context.

These particulars indicated that the document had aged, some parts of it less gracefully than others. More important, however, was the overall nature of the 1976/79 guidelines. They include the ringing statement that "the feature of information service, irrespective of its level or intensity, is to provide an end-product in terms of information sought by the user."[6] This statement places the user in a central position; however the rest of the document, at least implicitly, regulates the user of a library's information service to a secondary role. Overall the 1976/79 guidelines are more concerned about facilities, collections, and management of services than about the beneficiaries of the services. Admittedly, all of these things must be tended to in order to serve users. However the document as a whole does not give users a central role, a deficiency made most evident in the model outline for a service policy manual. There users are considered only *after* statements about the purpose of the service and a lengthy taxonomy of types of service. Clearly, this was a document that in 1988 needed not fine tuning by major revision.

CLIMATE OF THE LATE 1980s

The climate of the late 1980s when revision began in earnest included not only elements of the discontent analyzed by Bunge and Miller, but also a very different situation for public, academic, and special libraries. Publishers have always sought to avoid the middleman of the library and sell their information products directly to users. However some products, notably indexing and abstracting services for periodicals, had never lent themselves to the same sort of direct marketing and sales as books and journal subscriptions.

Online access to these through somewhat user-friendly search systems such as BRS AfterDark and DIALOG's Knowledge Index changed matters in the 1980s. Through these systems users could purchase just that small part of the indexing or abstracting service that they needed for a particular project—just the little they needed, no more, no less. In other words, they no longer needed to go to the library nor to depend upon the library for this sort of information. They could also turn to online systems for directory information—only that which they needed rather than the national coverage delivered between the two covers of a book—at a cost far below that of an annual subscription to an expensive business directory in printed form.

Advertisers are rarely accused of telling the truth, the whole truth, and nothing but the truth. It is not surprising then, that vendors and others made exaggerated claims for online services. Personal computing magazines of the 1980s were cheerleaders for these services, promising their readers they could get all of the information they needed right from their homes if they had a microcomputer, modem, software, and phone line. In effect, they were claiming that the library had become superfluous in the personal computer age. This continues in 1990 in direct mail marketing. A direct mail solicitation to become a user of Sears' online PRODIGY® service invites the prospective user to "consider the PRODIGY service to be *your personal one-stop source* for information."[7] This line of thinking is mere wishfulness, undermined by the fact that most information sources are *not* available online. Like the reports of Mark Twain's death, these implicit obituaries for the book were and are exaggerations.

In any community, whether that community is a school, a corporation, a college or university, or a municipality, the greatest single concentration of information sources is in its library. Only the library takes upon itself the responsibility to collect or provide access to information sources in all media—print, online, microform, CD-ROM, audiovisual, etc.—and to make these available to the members of the local community to fulfill their information needs. What the online vendors have to sell isn't so much information (much of it already available in or through the library in print, online, or CD-ROM) as convenience. Along with that convenience, however, can go a false sense of confidence in the sufficiency of the online service when it is, in fact, a channel to but a small fraction of the information available on most subjects. Nevertheless, the growing popularity of online services among end users has underscored the importance and validity of the statement that information services exist "to provide an end-product in terms of information sought by the user." Libraries, if truly attuned to users' needs can fulfill those needs more effectively than any other single source no matter how convenient to the user. The vision of the "library without walls," the brainchild of technological advances in telecommunications, has yet to be realized. The 1976/79 RASD guidelines, very much concerned with the library as place and structure, intimate at best a dim awareness of a model of the library as a service organization reaching beyond its walls and being reached from beyond its walls. The reality for the 1990s is that the library will become more and more place in which services for remote users are based. It is too early to say if this is a transitional phase. Until another medium replaces the book, it seems unlikely that the library as structure and place or the library's services to on-site users will wither. Rather the library must change to accommodate the service patterns that technological advances have made and will continue to make possible.

NEW GUIDELINES ADOPTED IN 1990

To meet the changed conditions of this environment the 1976 guidelines had to be updated. And they have been. The RASD Board of Directors adopted "Information Services for Information Consumers: Guidelines for Providers" in June 1990.[8] Reference librarians in every type of library should consider this an occasion for regenerative June joy to bust out all over their reference rooms, their OPACs, their modems, their CD-ROMS, their FAX boards, their NREN proposals, and even the bound volumes of *Reader's Guide to Periodical Literature* and the *Guide to Reference Books*, for they will need all of these tools to provide quality information service during the decade ahead. The winter of discontent for reference librarians had been giving way to a thaw as they had become more accustomed to the challenges of integrating technology into formerly manual processes and of juggling the command languages of various online systems. It gave way to a full blown, joyful, sunny summer in Chicago in June of 1990 when "Information Services for Information Consumers: Guidelines for Providers" superseded the outdated "A Commitment to Information Services: Developmental Guidelines."

A NEW VISION FOR SERVICES

"Information Services for Information Consumers: Guidelines for Providers" offers librarians a new vision for information services. The guidelines were deliberately written as a set of ideals to be worked towards rather than as a codification of the practice of the late 1980s. The subcommittee charged with revising "Commitment" chose this approach because it hoped to create a document that would stand the test of time better than "Commitment" did twelve years after its adoption and because of its members' desire to challenge librarians to think and act boldly about the ways in which they can incorporate new technology into their work. It also envisions a proactive form of information services, as concerned from its very first sentence to its last with such a service's potential users as with those who seek it out. Librarians who take these guidelines to heart will find themselves experimenting with new services, seeking out underserved groups, and testing various allocations of their resources to achieve the best mix of services for the respective communities they serve.

The introductory paragraph of the 1990 guidelines firmly acknowledges the continuing role of the library as place and, more importantly, as a collection of information sources in various media. It also notes that "because it possesses and organizes for use its community's single largest concentration of information resources," the library has an obligation to "develop information services appropriate to its community."[9] The guidelines never lose sight of the reasons for information services—the user and the user's information needs. Two of the few vestiges of the old "Commitment to Information Services" document discernible in "Information Services for Information Users" are the statements that "provision of information in the manner most useful to its clients is the ultimate test of all a library does"[10] and "the goal of information service is to provide an end-product: the information sought by the user."[11] These deliberately echo the 1976 statement that "the feature of information service, irrespective of its level or intensity, is to provide an end-product in terms of information sought by the user." However the 1990 statements go further.

Any document drafted by a subcommittee of an ALA divisional committee and then approved by the parent committee and the divisional board after solicitation of comments and an open hearing inevitably shows signs of improvement. It just as inevitably shows signs of compromise between the initial draft and the requests of other members or bodies of the division. "Information Services for Information Consumers" is no exception. In an early draft this key sentence read "provision of information in the form most useful to its clients is the ultimate test of all a library does." The word "form" alarmed some who thought that it might be interpreted to mean that information should be conveyed to a client in a particular medium. These respondents were uncomfortable with this notion because they feared it implied that a patron's preferences could override a library's policies, for example, that a library should fax a document to a patron rather than require the patron to come to the library and examine it on the premises. Changing the word to "manner" assuaged these fears. But, of course, the broader term "manner" includes the implications some were wary of. Delivering information in the "manner most useful" to a client can mean more than selecting the medium most convenient to the user (e.g., TDD, FAX, telephone call, etc.); it can also mean "massaging" the information into a form more useful to the client than the form in which it was retrieved from some information source. This could be as simple as sorting for the patron's convenience the results of an on-line search of a bibliographic database or as ambitious as preparing a digest and synthesis of a number of source documents. The more broadly and generously a library interprets this crucial statement, the more responsive its information service will be to its clients' needs. As the guidelines themselves note, "in applying the guidelines, library administrators and information services staff will need to emphasize those statements appropriate to their particular library, its mission, and the community it serves."[12] While the document changed as a result of the inevitable compromises of its approval process, the changes were more cosmetic than substantive. None of the revisions dimmed its vision of thorough, accurate, client-centered information service designed to meet the clients' needs thoroughly and in a way that places a higher premium on the client's convenience than the library's.

EFFORTS TO LIMIT THE VISION

Very few comments were submitted to the subcommittee during the comment and hearings phase of the adoption process. However most of those that were made can be characterized as requests to limit statements so that they would state readily attainable goals rather than the lofty goals proposed in the draft. No passage illustrated this pull of the gravity of present practice as clearly as the discussion of section 1.13 on referrals. In draft this read:

> When the library is not able to provide a client with needed information, it should refer that client to some other agency or an expert who can provide it. Such referrals should not be made, however, until after the information services personnel have confirmed that the agency or expert to whom the client is being referred can indeed provide the information and will extend its services to that user.

The objection to the latter part of this was that it was impractical to check on such matters before making a referral. The specific objection was that "in some situations that may not be necessary. For example, in a university library system with several branches, referrals between departmental libraries would not normally require the staff to confirm that the patron's specific request could be answered if the subject matter fell within that department's domain."[13] One can debate this; a university may embrace the universe of knowledge but that does not necessarily mean that its library system has captured all of that knowledge and neatly categorized it into discipline-specific branch libraries. The revised version of 1.13 preserves the original's commitment to the user and its insistance upon confirming the value of a referral before sending a patron to a branch library a few blocks away or, perhaps, to another city's or college's library many miles away. In fact, by offering the option to refer the question rather than the client, it shows even greater concern for the client's convenience. In final form, section 1.13 reads:

> When the library is not able to provide a client with needed information, it should refer either the client or the client's question to some other agency, an expert, or another library which can provide the needed information. Before referring a client to an agency, expert, or another library, information services personnel should confirm that the agency, expert, or library to which the client is being referred can indeed provide the information and will extend its services to that user. When a question is referred to another agency, the referring library should follow all local, state, regional, or national protocols in effect, including those governing selection of transmittal forms (e.g., the Information Request Form) and communications media.[14]

"Information Services for Information Consumers" consistently calls on libraries and librarians to provide services, even services nobody in a community has asked for, in a proactive manner. For example, the guidelines call on libraries to "add value" to information when "it is not immediately useful as presented in its source."[15] They state that a "library's building should not be a boundary to its information services;"[16] that "in anticipation of users' needs, the library should identify outside information systems, organizations, and individual experts it can call upon"[17] as needed; that "the library should support state-of-the-art communications methods for access to information resources for users, whether within or outside its building(s)."[18] In other words, the library should offer services that meet users' information needs present and future and take advantage of advances in communications technology to offer users options in access and delivery systems for those services.

AN OCCASION FOR JOY!

All of this ought to be occasion for June joy for reference librarians. Challenges such as these have the potential, of course, to induce stress. Stress from a variety of sources sent reference librarianship into its winter of discontent in the early 1980s. However the guidelines articulate a vision of information services shaped by users' needs, both expressed and unexpressed. It simply *must* be assumed that reference librarians' oft professed commitment to users is genuine. If it were not, the drop-out rate from the profession would be astronomical since the pecuniary awards alone are not sufficient to retain most people. That commitment in itself ought to ameliorate any new sources of stress encountered in an effort to implement the guidelines. Adoption of the guidelines provides librarians with an ideal impetus to examine policies governing information services to be sure that the policies promote rather than impede service to users.

Implementation of the guidelines will require creativity on the part of reference librarians and library administrators. They will have to experiment with new information services and new modes of service to determine what mix is the most appropriate for their respective communities, whether those communities are the students and faculty of a school or university, the citizens of a city or county, or the employees of a corporation or government agency. Risk is inherent in change. Librarians will have to become risk takers in order to bring the guidelines' vision to fruition. And if they are not already doing so, library administrators will have to nurture an institutional culture that promotes risk taking and that rewards success and that penalizes not the taking of a risk that fails, but the failure to risk at all. Senior administrators can allocate resources and middle managers can draw up plans, but the ultimate key to successful implementation of the guidelines will be individual reference librarians' commitment to the guidelines' spirit. Reference librarians work independently, usually alone, and without close supervision. Each one has numerous opportunities to interpret or ignore policy. Consensus among the librarians in a reference department is not a given. It may be a greater challenge for reference managers to gain endorsement of the guidelines by all staff members than to cajole sufficient funding from administrators to develop programs in the guidelines' spirit. Those who achieve unanimity and attain funding will have no end of opportunities to share their clients' joy over receiving the information they need in the form in which they need it when they need.

It remains to be seen how well "Information Services for Information Consumers" will stand the test of time. While its particular expression may come to look a bit tarnished, the ideals it expresses for a truly client-centered information services—that is, an information service devoted to providing clients with thorough, accurate information in a timely manner and in the medium of the client's choice—will continue to shine as brightly as the rejuvenating June sun that warms the spirits and quickens the blood of the young. If librarians take the guidelines to heart, both they and the information consumers for whom they provide information services will have plenty of reason year round to sing out that "Joy is bustin' out all over!"

REFERENCES

1. James Rettig, "Reference Services," in Robert Wedgeworth, ed., *The ALA Yearbook of Library and Information Services 1985* (Chicago: American Library Association, 1985), 239.

2. Charles Bunge, "Potential and Reality at the Reference Desk: Reflections on a 'Return to the Field,'" *Journal of Academic Librarianship* 10 (July 1984): 128-33. William Miller, "What's Wrong with Reference: Coping with Success and Failure at the Reference Desk," *American Libraries* 15 (May 1984): 303-306, 321-322.

3. A draft of the guidelines was published as "A Commitment to Information Services: Developmental Guidelines," *RQ* 14 (Fall 1974): 24-26. The version adopted by the RASD Board in January, 1976, was published as "A Commitment to Information Services: Developmental Guidelines," *RQ* 15 (Summer 1976):327-330. The final version, incorporating the added section on ethics and adopted by the RASD Board in January, 1979, was published as "A Commitment to Information Services: Developmental Guidelines," *RQ* 18 (Spring 1979):275-278.

4. Section 3.2, "A Commitment to Information Services: Developmental Guidelines," *RQ* 18 (Spring 1979):277.

5. Ibid., 278.
6. Ibid., 275.
7. PRODIGY® Interactive Personal Service sales brochure, 1990. Italics in original.
8. "Information Services for Information Consumers: Guidelines for Providers," *RQ* 30 (Winter 1990): 262-65.
9. "Introduction" to "Information Services for Information Consumers: Guidelines for Providers," 262.
10. Ibid.
11. Section 1.1, "Information Services for Information Consumers: Guidelines for Providers," 262.
12. "Introduction" to "Information Services for Information Consumers: Guidelines for Providers," 262.
13. Letter to author, January 1990.
14. Section 1.13, "Information Services for Information Consumers: Guidelines for Providers," 263.
15. Section 1.10, "Information Services for Information Consumers: Guidelines for Providers," 263.
16. Section 1.11, "Information Services for Information Consumers: Guidelines for Providers," 263.
17. Section 2.5, "Information Services for Information Consumers: Guidelines for Providers," 264.
18. Section 3.4, "Information Services for Information Consumers: Guidelines for Providers," 264.

The Fragile Allure of Reference

Paul Frantz

SUMMARY. In spite of sometimes difficult working conditions, reference services continue to have an allure, both for prospective and experienced librarians. This attraction is explained in terms of a number of factors, including the archetypal role of reference, the various roles public service librarians perform, the positive feedback they experience, the different work rhythm of a reference desk, and the "encounters with reality" the desk provides. Yet the allure is fragile, and the same factors that give the reference desk its attraction also threaten the pleasures it can provide.

In a recent survey of students enrolled in American library schools, the type of library position perceived as most desirable was reference services.[1] In a ranking of sixteen different types of positions, work at the reference desk was the preference of approximately twenty-nine per cent of the respondents, getting roughly twice as many votes as collection development and four times as many votes as cataloging.

There is then a definite allure about the reference desk. Not only library school students, but also working professionals have noted the rewards, or at least the potential for rewards, of answering somebody else's questions.[2]

Yet anyone who has worked a regular shift at a public service desk, who has indicated, for the tenth time that hour, where the telephone directories are; who has three telephone calls on hold and four people queued up to ask questions; and who, at that moment, learns the CD-ROM printer has again jammed—anyone who has

---

Paul Frantz is Coordinator of Library Instruction, Knight Library, University of Oregon, Eugene, OR 97403.

© 1991 by The Haworth Press, Inc. All rights reserved.

worked reference at all has encountered these obvious taints to that allure.

For the pleasures of reference are delicate and exist in a potentially hostile environment. Like marine life in a tidal zone, we reference librarians are buffeted by the very forces that give us our identity as professionals and sustain us in that role.

THE ARCHETYPAL ROLE

For many of us who visited libraries regularly when we were younger, the person sitting at the reference desk was the only professional librarian we ever saw. The technical services staff has always been beyond the public's ken. The primary model of a librarian for the general public is still the reference librarian. If our interest in becoming a librarian originated in the time we spent in libraries, if we conjectured that the atmosphere of a library would be a good one in which to work, our idea of what that work entailed may have been largely shaped by what we saw reference librarians doing.[3] At some point, we stepped back from our own information needs and considered the providers of information: "How do they know all that stuff? Could I know it, too?"

Thus, serving at the reference desk is what many of us originally conceived librarianship to be. (Of course, such a generalization is dangerous. The impulses to buy materials (i.e., acquisitions) and build up collections (i.e., collection development) may both seem as basic to a prospective librarian's conception of the profession as answering questions. Yet it still seems plausible that the reference librarian serves as the career prototype for most candidates entering the field.)

So when we find ourselves answering questions at the reference desk, we enact a reversal. We, the former patrons, have become the professionals; the askers of information have become the providers. There is a satisfaction in seeing ourselves become that which, earlier, we may have regarded with a certain awe. The reversal is never complete, of course. We continue to be patrons in other library situations, although our understanding of the librarian-patron interaction is now completely different.

A patron approaches the reference desk, prefaces his question by saying he's not sure the library can help him, and then gives the nature of his research. The librarian asks one more question and then walks over amongst a reference collection of 30,000 books and selects the one, the precise one, that will answer the patron's question. The patron shakes his head in amazement and asks, "Do you have all these books memorized or something?"

Surely there is an element of magic in the manner in which an experienced reference librarian uses a library's resources.[4] Magicians have sleight-of-hand and mirrors; reference librarians have classification systems and subject headings. The essential difference between the two professions is that the magician tries, at all costs, to remain mystical, to hide the source of his magic, while the reference librarian is happy, even considers it part of her responsibilities, to reveal how she performs her art.

With magic comes power. As reference librarians, we hold keys to unlock storehouses of information. We are in a position where we know things others, our clients, don't: in a business setting, that would be the very definition of power. And of those resources, we have the choice of communicating as much, or as little, as we want. Unlike the magician, who wishes his audience to leave delighted but mystified, the reference librarian is not satisfied until the patron is both enlightened and empowered.

When a patron gives to a reference librarian a sketchy citation, or even an incorrect one, and through various bibliographic tools the librarian is able, not only to provide a complete citation, but also determine which library in the country owns a copy of the work, that librarian is performing a process of induction very familiar to a detective piecing together a case from the flimsiest of evidence. This the librarian does over and over (and over) again.

The difference between the librarian's work and that of the detective's is that the librarian derives the satisfaction without the gory details and in a fraction of the time. We are quicker and cleaner.

This is perhaps the aspect of reference librarianship—solving a puzzle—whose capacity for pleasure is most apparent to the layperson. Those who enjoy finishing crossword puzzles or watching television quiz shows must regard librarians with envy: they get paid for solving riddles.

THE LIBRARIAN AS COUNSELOR

All public service librarians function as counselors when they relieve the anxiety and anguish of the patrons as they experience the library. In public libraries, patrons may ask reference librarians to recommend a book, either for themselves or for their children. As a client places confidence in a psychiatrist's knowledge of human personality, so the patron places trust in the librarian's knowledge of the collection. In academic libraries, the researcher comes to the reference desk when stuck, at a dead end, or unable to begin. The librarian counsels: he inquires as fully as possible into the need and recommends a strategy for action. Reference librarians get stuck people "unstuck."

Acting as counselors satisfies the impulse many librarians have to provide service to the public.[5] Librarianship is a service profession, as is medicine or the ministry, and nowhere is the service more immediate than at the reference desk. One difference between librarianship and other service professions is that the actual time we take in providing service to our clients is typically much shorter than that required by other professionals. Our reference interview may take at the most minutes, whereas a doctor's or social worker's or minister's counseling may involve many hours.

This short-lived counseling has, for the librarian, its attendant advantages and disadvantages. When we work with researchers, we usually learn only enough about their information needs to assist them gather information. Their research is often fascinating, and the contact we have with that research is likewise fascinating. But our involvement is necessarily limited. We cannot give our entire two hour shift at the reference desk to one person. So our encounters with researchers generally result in our working with a fascinating subject for a brief, but intense, period of time and then discarding it, letting the researcher go on with the hard work of synthesizing the information. That is, we participate in the process of discovery without expending the hours necessary to complete the work.

The disadvantage, of course, to this sampling of our patrons' research is that librarians may feel that the intellectual content of their work, at least at the reference desk, is always going to be superficial. It is as if research is a fruit that we librarians bring to ripeness, but of which we only taste, never eat. In addition, the doctor or social worker will usually see a conclusion to his or her work. The patient gets better or doesn't; the social worker's client improves his situation or doesn't. But most typically the reference librarian gives assistance to patrons, never finding out if the advice has been helpful or not.

Sometimes librarians do find out if the assistance they have provided has been helpful. Patrons will return to the reference desk and tell us personally that our counsel was exactly what was needed; or they will thank us through a letter; or, less frequently, they will acknowledge our helpfulness in a publication.

It is again the reference librarian who has more opportunities than anyone else in the profession for this positive feedback. Do catalogers ever hear from patrons who found their cataloging helpful to their research? Acquisition and collection development librarians, when they do deal with the public, generally hear complaints as to why the library's collection is deficient in some field or why the library can't order something as fast as the local bookstore. Reference librarians field complaints too, and, standing in the front ranks, get them about all areas of the library, even those they have no responsibility for. But we also receive kudos, often face to face. A patron who, moments before, was befuddled by or even hostile to the library, may very well embarrass us with gratitude when our advice, even very simple advice, saves him hours of needless work. Our work at the reference desk may be the only part of our job to receive such open, spontaneous feedback.

THE RELIEF OF RANDOMNESS

Reference librarians have little control over the nature of the questions they receive. They may work at a desk that is the first line of access for patrons entering the library and so receive both directional, reference, and even circulation questions. Or, in libraries where information desks filter out directional questions, they may receive only reference questions but in a wide variety of fields. Or, if reference librarians work in specific departments (e.g., Humanities, Social Sciences, etc.) they may receive reference questions only in certain disciplines. But whatever the potential for questions, librarians working at a public desk cannot control the nature of the questions they receive or the rate at which they are asked. They cannot say, "This hour I will take only business questions." Or, "I've got work to do, so I'll only take five questions this next hour."

Every question received is a surprise. It may be a question the reference librarian has never heard before or one she has heard a thousand times. But, usually, the question will have been impossible to predict.

The fact that reference librarians have so little control over the essence of their job—the questions they answer—is, paradoxically, one of the saving graces of their work. When reference librarians place themselves open to whatever comes along, they become a part of a work rhythm in needed contrast to the rest of their work day. For although our work off the reference desk may seem hectic and prone to unpredictable events, it is usually characterized by choice: we decide to write a letter, to make a phone call, to respond to one of several memos, to schedule a meeting, to attend a meeting. We rarely come to work in the morning and say, "I'll do whatever comes along and hits me." But that's exactly what we have to do at the reference desk. From the moment we step to the desk, we are "hit" by questions not of our choosing.

The work rhythm of the reference desk is not necessarily slower than our regular work rhythm; on the contrary and as every reference librarian knows, it may be considerably faster. It may be, in fact, intolerably frantic. Nor does the randomness of the reference desk necessitate helplessness on the part of the reference librarian. We still make many choices with each patron: how much time to devote to the question, which resources to call upon, whether to defer the question to a colleague. But for the two or three (or more) hours we work at the reference desk, we must let ourselves be open to the rhythms brought by our patrons and the environment of the desk, not the rhythms we are accustomed to imposing on ourselves during our remaining work hours.

In the randomness of the reference desk comes the psychic relief of temporarily letting go of control. The unpredictability of every patron and of the question he or she brings gives us a chance to relinquish, for a while, the tight grasp we like to think we have over our lives. This letting go satisfies us, because it inserts a rhythm of relaxation into a work rhythm that may tend towards firmly scheduled rigidity.[6] (If, however, the randomness becomes excessive — if we work too many hours at the desk, for instance — then the loss of control becomes not temporary, but entrenched, and our performance and job satisfaction deteriorate accordingly.)

The randomness of the reference desk, in a proper dosage, also provides necessary anxiety. Since we cannot know the nature of the next question, we cannot prepare its answer. Every question that is asked us is a test, a new test, for which we have only our experience to call upon. Recall your first week at a new reference desk, the trepidation with which you viewed the patrons walking up to you. There should be a faint remnant of that anxiety of the novice with every question received by the veteran librarian, years later. For it is the anxiety of being equal to the task that keeps us alert. Just as the concert pianist needs a few butterflies, even though it is the hundredth time she has played a concerto, and just as the lecturer needs to feel a little jittery before delivering a talk to the audience, so the reference librarian needs the necessary nervous tension in approaching the reference interview.

Librarians are fond of touting serendipity to patrons as a complement to more organized forms of research. Seldom do librarians realize that serendipity, this encounter with the fortuitous, comes to them also, at the reference desk, and that it is the spice of their work.

It may be argued that no other worker in the library gets to know people as well as the reference librarian, with the possible exception of the circulation librarian, who is able, after a few months on the job, to write a monograph on the causes of forgetfulness.

Reference librarians learn very quickly the gamut of personality types. One of my first work experiences was at a large public library on the West Coast, where the city's mental health officers counseled their clients to go to the downtown library if they felt any anxiety. Consequently, I would meet cases like the young man who rushed up to me and yelled, "You think you're Mozart, don't you! You're not! I am!" and then ran off in high glee. Or the woman, of whom we had been warned in advance, who would ask for books in storage, follow us back into the storage shelving, and then take off her clothes.

The reference librarian meets the hostile patron, for whom no service is ever performed adequately; the gracious patron, who never forgets to thank us; the stuttering patron, for whom the act of asking a question is an ordeal; and the gushing patron, who wants to tell us her life story as a prelude to her question. The reference librarian meets the introvert and the extrovert, the gifted and the disabled, the curious and the indifferent. And although many of these individual contacts may not be pleasant, the sum of a librarian's experiences with the public provides a gestalt of human nature that has the power to enrich or embitter.

For, as always, the pleasures of reference are accompanied by dangers. The obvious threat in our dealings with the public is the burnout associated with the hostility and indifference patrons can bring to the reference desk and to our efforts to assist them. The not so obvious menace is the assault on our own view of human nature that arises from constantly answering questions. At the reference desk, we typically see people at less than their best. We see them as struggling individuals, who reveal themselves as clumsy or ignorant in activities that we can do in our sleep. If we have spent too many hours on the desk, we can begin to develop a contempt for our patrons' ignorance of research activities we may consider instinctual: use of a card catalog, interpreting a citation, finding a book on the shelf. ("You can't do that? How stupid can you get!") We may begin to consider our fellow human as an idiot, unable to perform the simplest of operations and unappreciative of the "noble" help we can give.

If reference work keeps a public service librarian out of the ivory tower, then it can also put library administrators or library school educators—those in need of a glimpse of reality—in touch with the needs of patrons.[7] The inadequacies of a library become quickly apparent from the working side of a reference desk. Insufficient signage, an understaffing of a public service desk, a confusing system of finding periodicals, and the cumulative effect of answering forty questions an hour take on a new significance to the administrator or professor who works a few shifts at a reference desk.

THE REFERENCE DESK AS "CATCHALL"

A list of what reference desk librarians do when the desk is not busy would be endless, but here's a beginning: they sort through acquisition slips, read the newspaper, read a professional journal, read a magazine, watch people, read a novel, scan the recent additions to the reference collection, write poetry, write memos, develop handouts, talk to their partner at the desk, straighten the books on the index tables, or skim through their mail.

Reference librarians may feel guilty about some of the above activities, as if they should be doing something "more constructive," as if working at the reference desk and experiencing pleasure were two separate activities. This essay has tried to contend that work and pleasure are *not* two contradictory events, especially at the reference desk. Therefore, the numerous "catchall" activities reference librarians bring to the desk are not out of line, so long as two guidelines are kept in mind.

First, in his role as counselor, the reference librarian needs to remember the service priority of the reference desk. If his posture at the desk leads a patron to ask, "Are you busy?" or "Pardon me for interrupting," then the librarian should realize that whatever activity he was doing has interfered with his first responsibility: to serve the public.

Second, reference librarians should be careful not to impose the ordered, carefully scheduled rhythm of the rest of their working day on the reference desk, which has, as we have seen, an entirely different work mode, that of randomness. A librarian at a public service desk who expects to sort through her mail, work on a handout, and read the morning paper during her shift is asking too much of herself and expecting too little from her patrons. When we overlay our own schedule over the randomness of reference, we invite irritation and impatience, especially at those times when the traffic at the desk is fairly light, for then we are constantly shifting between the work we have brought to the desk and the work our patrons bring us.[8] We do neither justice and so get irritated at both. We deprive ourselves of the pleasure of reference.

Two recent trends in improving reference services have been the introduction of CD-ROMs into reference areas and the rethinking of "reference on demand," away from the notion that patrons should expect their questions, especially complex reference questions, to be answered immediately by someone sitting at the reference desk.

Patrons experience CD-ROMs as marvelous innovations in using periodical indexes, freeing them from constraints of cost and the nuisance of scheduling appointment searches with librarians. Reference librarians, on the other hand, may have a more mixed reaction to CD-ROMs.[9] In libraries where CD-ROM workstations stand without student or clerical attendants, reference librarians may spend as much time logging on the workstations, changing ribbons, discs, and paper, and fixing jammed printers as they do advising patrons on search strategies. In terms of the allure of reference, the librarian's role as counselor and magician is diminished to that of clerk. In particular, the reference librarians' pride that theirs is a skill few other professionals possess is directly threatened when technological innovations inadvertently replace their "magical" activities with clerical. The advent of more and more workstations into the reference area are accompanied by librarians commenting, "I didn't spend two years in library school to fix printers!" Likewise, the replacement of librarian-mediated online searching with CD-ROM searching reduces the opportunities for librarians to work with patrons for extended periods of time and become involved in their research.

The second innovation in reference services—deemphasizing the centrality of the reference desk through the use of technology—has likewise arisen from obvious reference limitations. Patrons and reference librarians alike have long been frustrated with trying to deal with complex, lengthy reference questions in the traditional reference desk, stand-in-line fashion. When a question requires fifteen minutes of work, why not give it fifteen minutes, instead of dealing with it superficially in three? And so have evolved several reference alternatives. Even the most traditional libraries have routines where paraprofessionals handle the questions they feel able to answer and refer the more difficult ones to reference librarians who schedule appointments with the patrons. More recent have been experiments in dealing with the questions of patrons by electronic mail, reference by computer, and artificial intelligence.[10] This technological assistance may alleviate the lines at the reference desk and give us more control over how we work most appropriately with our patrons, but it diminishes the role of randomness in reference. If carried to an extreme, where reference by appointment replaces entirely the traditional reference desk exchange, then reference becomes a series of entries in our desk calendars. Questions are never unexpected, their variety may be replaced by more homogeneity (as business questions are referred to the business librarian, etc.), and the psychic relief I have discussed earlier of a different mode or rhythm of work, of temporarily letting go of some of our control, is lost.

It is not that CD-ROMs and expert systems are inimical to the pleasures of traditional reference service. New systems promise new allures: first, CD-ROMs offer librarians the opportunity to convey the "magic" of online searching to many more patrons than through mediated searching; second, in the first stages of CD-ROM deployment, librarians and patrons may find themselves working together on learning how to master the individual searching protocols, and so enter into a different librarian-patron relationship, away from "magic" and into shared learning; and third, the use of computers to answer less difficult questions frees librarians to work more frequently in their role as counselors with patrons who really need their expert assistance. At the same time, it needs to be appreciated that any new technology, depending on how it is introduced into the library, has the power either to diminish or enhance the sense of professionalism of its employees. In addition, no matter how smoothly a technology is installed, some losses in job satisfaction may result (e.g., the randomness of reference) to be replaced by yet unforeseen pleasures.

Any improvements in library services, then, must be considered not only in terms of how services to patrons are enhanced but also how the satisfaction librarians receive in their work environment is maintained. For the allure of reference, while substantial, is very fragile and lives in a delicate balance with the demands librarians and their patrons make upon it.

REFERENCES

1. See William E. Moen and Kathleen M. Heim, "The Class of 1988: Librarians for the New Millenium," *American Libraries* 19 (November 1988), pp. 858-860, 885.

2. For two expressions of this, see Charles A. Bunge, "Potential and Reality at the Reference Desk: Reflections on a 'Return to the Field,'" *Journal of Academic Librarianship* 10 (July 1984), pp. 128-132; and Nathan M. Smith and David T. Palmer, "Reference: Rewards or Regrets, Believing Makes it so," *The Reference Librarian* 16 (Winter 1986), pp. 271-281.

3. See Moen and Heim, op. cit., p. 860, where approximately sixty-two per cent of the survey's respondents cited working librarians as influencing them to become librarians.

4. For an analysis of this "magic," see Caroline Spicer, "The Reference Mystique," *Cornell University Libraries Bulletin* 183 (May 1973), pp. 4-5.

5. See Moen and Heim, op. cit., p. 865, where approximately sixty-six per cent of the survey's respondents listed service orientation as a factor in their choice of library and information science work.

6. For two analyses of an "overcontrol" hypothesis, see James R. Averill, "Personal Control Over Aversive Stimuli and its Relationship to Stress," *Psychological Bulletin* 80 (October 1973), pp. 286-303, which specifies conditions in which control is stress inducing rather than reducing; and Judith Rodin, Karen Rennert, and Susan K. Solomon, "Intrinsic Motivation for Control: Fact or Fiction?" in Andrew Baum and Jerome E. Singer, eds., *Advances in Environmental Psychology, Volume 2: Applications of Personal Control* (Hillsdale, NJ: Erlbaum, 1980), pp. 131-148. The impact of too much randomness on job performance is well documented. For one of the latest explorations, see David B. Greenberger et al., "The Impact of Personal Control on Performance and Satisfaction," *Organizational Behavior and Human Decision Processes* 43 (February 1989), pp. 29-51.

7. For the impressions of one library school professor who returned to the reference desks of both an academic and public library, see Bunge, op. cit.

8. See Averill, op. cit.

9. For a survey contrasting general acceptance by users with mixed reactions from librarians, see Kristine Salomon, "The Impact of CD-ROM on Reference Departments," *RQ* 28 (Winter 1988), pp. 203-219.

10. See "Expert Systems in Reference Services," *The Reference Librarian* 23 (1989); and Barbara J. Ford, "Reference Beyond (and Without) the Reference Desk," *College and Research Libraries* 47 (September 1986), pp. 491-494.

Reference Collegiality: One Library's Experience

Polly Frank
Lee-Allison Levene
Kathy Piehl

SUMMARY. The cooperation and collegiality that can be a part of providing reference service bring joy to reference librarians fortunate enough to work in such an environment. This article examines the benefits one reference staff has found in attempting to maintain a collegial atmosphere. Collegiality contributes to building a positive daily environment, sharing responsibility for completion of special reference projects, and fostering professional and personal growth. By stressing cooperative efforts, reference staff members have broadened their skills in areas such as online searching and collection development. Librarians have increased their professional involvement through publication and conference participation. They have undertaken major cooperative efforts in projects such as weeding. Above all, they experience daily satisfaction in working with a team of professionals interested in providing quality reference service.

In a society in which competition rather than cooperation is stressed and individuals often seek their own professional advancement at others' expense, the collegiality involved in providing quality reference service can bring joy. During the past four years, reference librarians at Mankato State University have derived numerous benefits from increasing efforts at cooperation. This paper will explore the ways in which collegiality contributes to creat-

---

Polly Frank, Lee-Allison Levene, and Kathy Piehl are reference librarians at the Memorial Library, Mankato State University, Mankato, MN 56001.

ing a positive work environment, completing special projects, and fostering professional and personal growth.

Anyone who has worked in a college or university can describe how zealously some faculty members guard their turf. Such professors meet their classes, maintain the minimum number of required office hours, then disappear to pursue their own research or other interests. They maintain almost no contact with individual colleagues or the department as a whole. Subject specialization and strict division of labor make such solitary pursuit of an academic career possible in traditional teaching departments.

The same structure works much less well in an academic library, especially a reference department in which all librarians are required to staff a general reference desk. During a two-hour desk assignment, the librarian might be called upon to handle requests for information on topics ranging from business to children's literature to nursing. Without pooling knowledge and expertise, the reference staff's ability to serve the public depends on having each librarian try to master all subject areas, a formidable task.

However, four years ago, reference staff members at Mankato State found themselves in almost that position. Tasks were divided among the full-time reference librarians, assisted by one clerical staff person and numerous student workers. Compartmentalization of duties resulted in low levels of interaction on a daily basis or even during scheduled meetings.

One reference librarian assumed major responsibility for performing database searches scheduled by faculty and graduate students. Two librarians accepted the task of developing and maintaining the entire reference collection. Although they encouraged suggestions from other staff members, they initiated most of the orders. One reference librarian concentrated on interlibrary loan. Other necessary reference activities were divided similarly. Almost all scheduled library instruction was provided by librarians in a separate bibliographic instruction unit, which was not linked to the reference group in any formal way.

The provision of reference service reflected a similar independence as well as a type of siege mentality in which patrons needed to make an effort to seek librarians' assistance. The physical arrangements and reference desk staffing contributed to this situation.

Reference librarians worked behind an L-shaped counter in an area that housed an extensive collection of reference books used in answering questions. Because patrons could not enter the room to look at the books, they needed to request items from a librarian and then check out the materials to use in the library.

Except for hours such as early morning or late evening, two librarians staffed the reference area. If someone was gone due to illness, vacation, or professional obligations, the other librarian assigned that desk hour often worked alone. Although some consultation occurred in answering difficult questions, the degree of cooperation varied a great deal. Librarians had to make a special effort to move around the counter to interact with patrons once they had requested help.

COOPERATION

Four years later we have moved out to patrons both physically and psychologically. One reference/information station is situated in the catalog room and one in the reference room. Almost all the reference books that were housed behind the counter have been returned to the reference stacks or moved out to a much smaller ready reference collection accessible to patrons as well as librarians. Although a greater geographic distance separates the two reference librarians on duty, we make the effort to contact each other for advice, to walk with patrons from one area to another, to move around looking for people who need help.

When we know we will be unable to work during a scheduled desk hour, we make arrangements for another librarian to work that time so that a single librarian isn't left to scramble through an hour alone. If an illness or emergency makes last-minute substitutions necessary, the rest of the staff members pitch in to cover the desk hours. All reference librarians share the responsibility for ordering materials for specific subject areas of the reference collection. We have expanded the number of hours during which reference service is provided. More librarians are involved in database searching and in instruction. In fact, the bibliographic instruction unit has been incorporated into reference.

In short, group involvement has replaced isolated activity. To a large extent we have overcome our reluctance to admit our lack of knowledge about a specific reference tool or an entire subject area. Instead of trying to cover up our weaknesses, we can seek out another librarian with expertise in a subject area and ask for help without fear that our colleague will make us feel stupid.

When a librarian prepares a bibliographic instruction session in a particularly complex area, she often takes time in a reference meeting to alert the rest of the librarians about the imminent assignment and to review materials that will be useful in helping the students. Each week one reference librarian spends five to ten minutes explaining the features of a reference tool that she has found particularly useful.

The exchange of information and the establishment of a common goal of providing high quality reference service create a positive daily atmosphere. The generally high level of trust and comfort is apparent in our willingness to laugh at ourselves. Summarizing the events of the day, one librarian recalled that she had noticed an unusually cheerful student grinning to herself as she happily typed away on a new CD-ROM index. When a class came along for a CD-ROM demonstration, the librarian turned to speak to the student, expecting to set the stage for an upbeat instructional session. "You've been searching this index for some time this morning. How do you like it?" the librarian asked. Much to her surprise the student beamed and cheerfully replied, "So far, not very much!" During particularly busy and muddled days, sharing our humorous encounters reduces stress and boosts our community spirit.

Special celebrations occur both during the workday and outside of regular work hours. We have the usual birthday celebrations and baby showers, of course. But we have also held "project completion" parties and one day had a chocolate chip cookie feast in honor of the reference coordinator's accomplishment of a major goal: clearing off her desk!

Outside of work hours, groups of librarians go out to dinner, attend plays, or hold potlucks. Although we all have other friends and activities in the community, we enjoy each other's company enough to spend time together outside the library. When one of the librarians had an exhibit of her paintings shown at a local gallery, her colleagues attended the opening reception to give her support and encouragement despite the fact that the temperature outside was over 100 degrees, and the building that housed the exhibit had no air-conditioning!

REASONS FOR CHANGE

How and why have these changes occurred during the past four years? The climate for change had started to be established a year earlier when a new library director arrived. After looking at the work environment, he decided that one of his goals would be increased cooperation among the library staff.

When faculty sabbatical leaves necessitated the hiring of replacement personnel, a possibility for change materialized. Four librarians were added on a temporary basis. All had at least half their time assigned to the reference area. Having a significant number of new people join the library faculty at once had an immediate impact. The average length of time librarians had been at Mankato State was over 15 years. No one had been hired for a tenure-track position in more than 5 years. Only two people had joined the staff in part-time or noncontinuing positions since then.

The arrival of a number of new people automatically changes group dynamics, and due to sabbatical leaves and staff shifts, the number of newly-hired reference librarians nearly equalled the number of reference veterans. What could have resulted, of course, was a division into two camps with endless disputes about reference approaches and philosophies.

However, several factors helped us avoid that scenario. First, there were some veterans ready to move toward a more cooperative model of reference service. Instead of blocking suggestions for change, they supported initiatives that led to more group interaction. Without their willingness to experiment with different ways of providing reference service, prospects for cooperative ventures would have been dim.

The second key element was that one of the four temporary positions was filled by an excellent reference librarian from another university who had decided to take a leave to participate in and study reference service at a different academic library. Her insights and suggestions proved invaluable because she combined years of reference experience with a newcomer's perspective. During her year at Mankato, she advocated and began several projects that drew the reference staff together.

A third factor fostering a cooperative reference environment can only be described as luck. Because the job possibilities in Mankato for librarians had been dismal for several years, the community contained a group of librarians who were eager for a chance to put their skills to work in an academic library. The delight in having professional positions and the desire to prove their value for the library's programs and services motivated the newcomers to work hard and establish places for themselves as quickly as possible. Antagonizing the librarians on the permanent staff would not have been in their best interests.

Besides assigning all four librarians to one area of the library in the hope of promoting change, the director also began a collection development initiative involving all library faculty. Because much of this work with academic departments was new to everyone, the project put all librarians on an equal footing as they attempted to devise ways to analyze the collection and communicate with other faculty on campus. Librarians from many parts of the building established informal work groups, and although some of the communication among librarians involved expressions of frustration about the overwhelming new tasks, at least people had a mutual point of discussion.

Within the reference area, work with the collection became the first step toward group efforts in a number of other areas. The first project involved an assessment of the large collection of reference books kept behind the desk by librarians who used the works in answering questions.

READY REFERENCE EVALUATION

The reference staff undertook the evaluation of our massive ready reference collection with the hope of achieving two goals: making as many sources as possible available directly to the library user and decreasing the burden on the librarians of handling a reserve operation. Over the years librarians had insinuated their favorite titles, books that required a long walk to retrieve, heavily used items, books prone to theft, or reference materials on little-known topics into this collection. Ready reference was no longer "ready" but bulky and cumbersome. The collection sat on shelves behind a service counter staffed by two reference librarians and an occasional workstudy student. The counter created an effective barrier requiring library patrons to ask for a title if they wanted to use it. The size of this collection—twenty-five shelves—struck terror in the heart of any new librarian, who would spend weeks memorizing titles on the shelves. It was time for a change.

First we had to arrive a consensus on a definition of ready reference and next decide how to conduct our evaluation. The criteria for ready reference covered six areas: special tools of the library trade, basic compendia, major sources to answer frequently asked questions, up-to-date directories, indexes to frequently sought information, and security for heavily used reference works.

Once the librarians agreed to the working definition of the six areas, our difficult task started. At our weekly reference staff meeting, we considered a cart of ready reference titles and discussed each one, title by title. Our group agreed that consensus was necessary to determine if a title should remain in the ready reference collection or return to the regular reference shelves. It was also understood that each librarian could keep one favorite title whether it fit the definition or not.

This weekly item-by-item discussion continued over four months until the ready reference collection was reduced by half. The visible result of this project was a manageable ready reference collection. The invisible benefits were imbedded in the group process. The evaluation began with some librarians worried about the integrity of the collection and their personal power in the reference group. We finished with the reference librarians satisfied with the titles sent back to the reference shelves and a sense of mutual respect, individual power intact. We were well on the way to accomplishing our goals.

The first group project set the stage for our next effort. Mankato State University's Library has an OPAC developed by the Project for an Automated Library System, commonly referred to as PALS. The library technical and clerical staff members were making a systematic, collection-by-collection effort at entering all library materials into PALS. The library did this by barcoding each item, which entails applying a zebra code and entering basic information into the automated system. No one could remember an orderly review of the reference holdings for superseded materials, duplications, outdated items, and titles that were falling apart. As a group we opposed barcoding the reference collection before completing a thorough review and weeding. A subcommittee of reference librarians formed and met regularly, producing documents filled with procedures and policies. The net result was that five months after our initial evaluation of ready reference, the staff was ready, once again, for a major group project. The librarians chose a procedure for weeding that changed how reference collection development was handled. Each librarian, based on subject expertise or interest, took areas to weed. We agreed to be responsible for developing whatever areas we weeded. Our goal, quite unrealistic, was to finish our first sweep through the reference collection in one month. Even though this was a quick and dirty first run, we underestimated how long it would take to read hundreds of prefaces, something at which we became experts.

The librarians set aside most regular commitments except for our assigned reference duties. We developed a color coding process used in conjunction with specially developed evaluation slips, telling any inquisitive librarian the future disposition of a specific title. All items that reference planned to discard or move to another area in the library were available for review by all library staff for a week. Librarians from other areas walked through once to reassure themselves that we were acting responsibly. The reference coordinator consulted with librarians from other floors about materials reference thought appropriate for their areas.

One ground rule was, when in doubt, retain it; another was, respond positively when a colleague questions your decisions. This process reinforced what started with the ready reference evaluation: we listened to one another and trusted each other's judgments. We had to trust ourselves and our colleagues' professional abilities because the task at hand was massive. We discovered that each of us, even with weeding guidelines, approached the process differently. This was the beginning of the reference librarians' taking responsibility for a portion of the collection, and that felt good. Two months after setting this process in motion, the majority of the project was finished. Reference now had a tighter, usable reference collection that was ready for the barcoders to enter each item into PALS.

DATABASE SERVICES

These two cooperative efforts led the way for continued change in the reference area. Two months after finishing weeding reference, another librarian began changes in how we offer database searching. Previously a few well-trained librarians conducted database searching by appointment only. Two or three one-hour slots were available Monday through Friday. There was a need for a low cost, quick and dirty database search aimed at the undergraduate preparing a speech or writing a composition paper. Reference offered this service at a set hour Monday through Friday on a first come, first served basis. For $2.00 we provided twenty-five or fewer citations from a Wilson database. In order to give this service, the number of searchers expanded. There were librarians doing Quicksearch who had no formal training as database searchers; the pool spread into technical services, bibliographic instruction, and beyond. We wanted individuals that showed interest and were willing to commit the time to searching and maintaining their skills. This provided an opportunity for "rusty" searchers to brush up their techniques while inexperienced searchers had a chance to test their abilities in a low-risk situation. Quicksearch was a tremendous success; we were inundated. This service changed as charges to our library increased. Each search now costs a dollar more for fifteen or fewer citations. In order to be responsive to student needs, reference developed a drop off, 24-hour turn-around Quicksearch service.

For the past year, a committee whose primary focus is the developing technology and impact of CD-ROM, met regularly. The majority of the librarians on this committee worked in reference with key people from other areas in the library also involved. Because of the noticeable changes occurring in reference and their effects library-wide, maintaining good collegial relationships throughout the library is also important. Cooperative committees promote this vital contact. Librarians are currently monitoring the effect of CD-ROM technology on Quicksearch, regular database searching, interlibrary loan, and other services.

At the same time Quicksearch evolved, the reference librarians participated in brainstorming sessions on how to improve other reference services. We had a no-holds-barred session with every idea presented up for consideration. This meeting resulted in a number of physical changes providing greater patron access to librarians and several collections. Simultaneously, due to a new, meticulous library technician, there was a reorganization behind the scenes, including rearrangement of librarian desk space and our interlibrary loan operation.

In order to implement the changes the reference staff wanted, we needed another evaluation of the ready reference collection. This time our collection was to be moved from behind the counter to a double section of rolling shelving, accessible to library patrons. Our first task was identification of reference items assigned for class use. Those stayed behind the counter for security. The second evaluation of ready reference, unlike the first, was accomplished in two weeks with little discussion because we trusted each other and were committed to change. Therefore, a month after implementing Quicksearch, ready reference came out from behind the formidable counter. At the same time, our zip code and telephone book collections were relocated. These had previously been behind the counter also, constantly monitored and dispensed by librarians.

Next came our most dramatic step. Instead of working behind an L-shaped waist-high counter covering more than 16 feet, the reference librarians moved out into the space where most questions occur, leaving a workstudy student behind the counter to manage the reference reserve materials and interlibrary loan items. One librarian was stationed in a room dominated by PALS terminals and numerous indexes and abstracts. The other librarian had a desk in an area with the remainder of the indexes and abstracts, ready reference, and the bulk of the reference collection. We decided to make this change on a trial basis, re-evaluating six months later in the fall. When the vote came, the librarians unanimously supported the new arrangement.

Simultaneously, a change happened in reference scheduling. Previously, the reference coordinator scheduled the first floor reference stations, using the librarians from that area. Another reference station on the third floor was scheduled by the third floor coordinator, using librarians from second and third floors. That spring, the reference coordinator, with help from the third floor coordinator, took over scheduling all three stations from 7:45 a.m. until 10 p.m., Monday through Friday. The group agreed to an exchange, that is third floor librarians on first and vice versa. This change exposed the first floor librarians to collections that were our most active referral points from the first floor: government documents, maps, microforms, and periodicals. And the second and third floor librarians renewed their acquaintance with familiar reference tools and discovered new titles.

BIBLIOGRAPHIC INSTRUCTION

That fall, as we decided to keep the new reference configuration, there were changes afoot in the bibliographic instruction unit. In another lifetime bibliographic instructions was part of reference, and then the units separated. The instructions librarians handled most of the classes, except specialized topics for which classroom teachers contacted specific librarians directly. Since two of the instruction librarians had shared appointments with reference, we decided to reintegrate the two units.

The next step was expansion of the pool of potential instructors for these one- and two-hour, one-time-only sessions. In order to make this change, the "guilt board" had to be eliminated and replaced with a better system. This bulletin board resided in the bibliographic instruction office. It showed who was teaching what, when and which classes were pending and needed someone from bibliographic instruction to do them. In essence, whoever felt guiltiest took the class. We needed a more equitable distribution system. First the guilt board went to surplus, and a system for class assignments using a central scheduler started. Next, all librarians received questionnaires asking for their weekly schedule. They indicated their desk hours, regular meetings, and times off. On another sheet the librarians listed their strengths and weaknesses, what they felt capable of teaching and subjects for which they would rather die than teach. Not everyone is capable of or interested in teaching. Those who did not want to be part of the instruction pool could sign up for scheduled library tours or demonstrations of PALS. Librarians with assignments in bibliographic instruction formed the core group of instructors. The additional pool allowed distribution of classes by specialty and provided a chance to take some of the overload off the core group.

Because of retirements, resignations, and internal reassignment of professional staff members, three of the four librarians hired four years ago have remained at Mankato State as part of the reference group. The fourth returned to her permanent position at another university at the end of her sabbatical. When other temporary and continuing positions in reference and instruction have occurred during the past four years, we have discussed our collegial philosophy and expectations with each person who came for an interview. We try to let prospective librarians know that they will be expected to contribute to the group effort in a number of ways.

In addition to the cooperative projects and evolution of services within our area that have benefitted the day-to-day reference service, we have experienced other intangible personal and professional gains. Listening to one another, we pay attention to our colleagues' research interests, professional questions, and dreams. Our successes have taught us how to encourage each other. We support the expressed interests of each librarian as well as the collective concerns of the group.

Near the beginning of each academic year, the reference group makes a list of collegial expectations. Bringing our expectations out in the open and naming individual concerns is not an easy task. Although members of the group occasionally have different points of view, sharing our opinions helps us understand each other and work toward a common goal. This procedure, involving the entire reference staff, builds trust and minimizes problems that turn up because of unspoken assumptions. As a result, we have agreed that we expect coworkers to post traded desk hours, develop the reference sections they weed, and relay phone messages promptly.

Another practice, at the end of the year, also nurtures our collegial community and gives closure to our efforts. The year-in-review report, given by our reference coordinator, celebrates our collective accomplishments. This litany of completed reference projects and jobs-well-done generates pride and encouragement and often makes us glad the year is over!

In addition to group support, librarians can count on individual support if we choose to reveal our personal and professional goals. As we read widely in our fields and attend a number of different conferences, coworkers often help each other connect with useful information. When we happen upon journal articles or opportunities for research or publishing that may be of interest to a coworker, we pass the information along. Frequently, librarians add comments to xeroxed copies of the articles referring colleagues to particularly noteworthy sections.

There is growing interest in attending conferences, specialized training programs, and continuing education sessions. Our interests draw us to state, regional, and national conferences and training in all areas of academic reference and information services, reference collection development, database searching, information technology, bibliographic instruction and numerous other specialized subject areas. Conferences extend our opportunities to make contacts for colleagues as well as ourselves. Recently, a publisher requested help from a librarian to review health science materials as a result of another librarian's networking efforts.

As the librarians take these opportunities to support one another's interests, respect and trust grow. A reciprocal form of mentoring has developed; we interact as informal role models. Recognizing that each librarian has special skills and areas of expertise, we share our strengths. A high trust level enables us to reveal our needs as well. We both ask and advise each other about reference interaction and communication, service provision, research, writing, collection development, and a variety of other skills.

Reciprocal mentoring means that a librarian will pair with a colleague to learn or improve on a skill and will, at some other time, switch hats and respond to her colleague's interest in an area she knows best. One librarian shared her legal research skills with a colleague who frequently provides writing and editing guidance. We seek opportunities to reciprocate for help received. The librarians pay attention to concerns expressed by colleagues and offer their knowledge or skills when appropriate.

Difficult reference questions bring us together at the reference desk to brainstorm search strategies. Frequently, a quick exchange between librarians, triggered by "have you thought about . . . " will initiate search ideas. Librarians working together on busy nights often find that they can handle questions faster when assisting each other in this way. When our colleagues request help, we respond, knowing they will help us when other tough reference questions are posed.

Hand-holding as novice database searchers, two librarians realized another level of reciprocal support. Determined to sink or swim, they shared their feelings of inadequacy and worked together. Practice, mutual back-patting, and some humor strengthened their skills as well as their respect for one another.

Skills are often modeled rather than taught. By observing our colleagues as team workers, team builders, communicators, organizers, and objective thinkers, we can identify specific behaviors we would like to emulate. After watching one librarian systematically organize her approach to her daily tasks, we talked about how it worked and why we thought it could work for us. Several librarians have followed her lead.

In a reciprocal mentoring environment, librarians learn by observation and modeling, informally pair with a colleague to improve a skill, and take turns giving in-house instructional sessions upon request. Informal guided walks, often led by the area developer, reacquaint the reference group with growing or complicated collections. Our "reference highlight," a 5 to 10 minute weekly informative talk, brings us together with librarians from other areas to learn about new services or special materials that would have an impact on reference service.

ADVANCED DEGREES

The collegiality of the reference environment nurtures short and long range personal and professional goals. With encouragement and support, several librarians have chosen to take classes to explore new interest areas, enter graduate programs, and finish advanced degrees. Each quarter, the library administration allows a limited amount of release time to take classes. During the past year, six out of seven members of the reference staff took advantage of the opportunity. An average of four librarians take at least one class each quarter.

Staff members often inquire about each others' classes, acknowledge accomplishments when they are shared, and support each other during test times. Our colleagues frequently offer to help us out and trade reference desk hours when tests or class projects cause time limitations. Encouragement from colleagues, with the added advantage of release time, helped two librarians pursue their second master's and two others continue work on their third master's degrees.

The reference librarians have shown greater interest in sharing their experience and research with others. More of us are presenting papers at conferences and writing and publishing articles. Our diverse interests have prompted us to give papers at children's literature, library and information technology, international business, reading, bibliographic instruction, and rural economic development conferences. The librarians offer to give feedback to colleagues who wish to practice their presentations and occasionally help each other edit papers and articles. The reference staff views individual success as team success.

Staff members look for professional opportunities for others as well as themselves and show growing interest in forming teams for research and writing. When a recent conference call for papers looked like an opportunity for a group presentation, librarians encouraged their colleagues from throughout the library to be part of the team. As a result of this process, one librarian acquired her first experience as a presenter at a conference and had a similar opportunity at another national conference later that year.

The collegial reference environment has also been influenced by temporary staff. In fact, librarians with short-term appointments and graduate assistants have made significant contributions to the reference community. A pivotal player worked with us for only a year. She contributed to the collegial environment by helping us recognize and nurture our individual and collective strengths. Two other short-term staff members worked especially well in our cooperative reference group. One offered gifts of time, surprising us at the reference desk to take our shifts when she thought we were especially busy. The other came to us as a graduate assistant to work full time on her second master's degree. She generously offered to team up with librarians who wished to improve their database searching skills and was particularly sensitive and encouraging to new learners. We have grown from our work with these "reference angels."

CONCLUSION

Throughout the past four years the collegiality and cooperative nature of reference at Mankato State University Memorial Library have grown. Increased communication and trust continue to nurture this environment with the one constant being change. We have successfully conducted group projects, changed services, implemented new procedures, grown personally and professionally, and continued to talk and struggle with one another.

Reference recognizes that new challenges lie ahead. As librarians leave and new staff members arrive, the chemistry changes. The library is also beginning a building expansion project that will take two noisy, cramped, and exciting years. Based on our experience of the past four years we expect the collegiality of the reference staff to survive.

Above one of our computer workstations is a poster of a group of African meerkats, small animals that live in communities. Part of the caption under their group portrait explains "They survive by sharing duties." That description applies to the reference staff as well.

Technology and Service: Reference Librarians Have a Place in the '90s

Mabel W. Shaw

SUMMARY. The future will be one of change driven by technology and information. Reference librarians are finding themselves in the forefront as information specialists committed to service to their users. With clients beginning to view librarians as essential professionals, there is a tremendous opportunity to combine well-designed services with the new technology and move into the role of assisting people to solve information problems. Successful programs will be centered around a user-oriented climate and provide access to a wide variety of information and technologies.

Reference librarians are working in a time of unparallel opportunities. A bold statement? Perhaps, but if ever there was a time for us to rejoice in our profession it is now, for we have a major role to play in an America where information is mass-produced the way automobiles once were. As we move toward the twenty-first century, we find ourselves serving as accessible and essential professionals in an information-demanding society.

Futurists speak of the quickening pace of change and the need to prepare oneself for a future that will be constantly in flux. In many fields this world is already a reality. Much of this change and development has taken place in the last two or three decades and may be attributed to the exponential expansion in the production of scientists that began with the Sputnik race. It is estimated that ninety percent of all scientists who have ever lived are alive today, and that

---

Mabel W. Shaw is Reference Librarian, Tallahassee Community College, 444 Appleyard Drive, Tallahassee, FL 32304.

as many scientific papers have been published in the forty years since 1950 as were published in all the centuries before this date.[1]

In the next ten to fifteen years, this pool of knowledge will double again. The driving force in this new age will not be manpower, machines, or manufacturing, but ideas, innovations, and information. Fueled by an ever-increasing ingress of research and development, the pace of new technology development is compressing product and process life cycles down to three to five years in many industries. As a result of this explosion of technology, change is accelerating at a dizzying pace.

In education, for example, this means that knowledge is transitory. The content students learn in their freshman classes will be outdated and replaced by the time they reach their second year on the job. There is little time for yesterday, today and tomorrow—there is only the "now." We are deluged with instant-everywhere and with it comes what Paul Simon calls " the staccato signals of information."[2]

Juxtapositioned with this emphasis on technological systems and information needs is an increased demand throughout all segments of our society for service. A recent issue of *Fortune* identified personal service as a key issue for the 1990s. Surveys of banking, high-tech, and manufacturing company customers found that these people consider "the personal touch" to be the most important aspect of their transactions. Another survey of 400 executives of the nation's largest companies identified "cares about the customer" as important as speed of delivery and convenience. Fast-food junkies at Burger King, who used to rank speed of service first, rank courtesy no. 1 today. Moreover, the customer wants personal service, the kind delivered by live bodies behind the sales counter, a human voice at the end of the telephone.[3]

REFERENCE LIBRARIANS—A CRITICAL FACTOR

Reference librarians, according to the literature, are "information specialists, information scientists, information brokers, information professionals, information gurus, guardians, gatekeepers."[4] Regardless of the title, we are becoming a critical factor in the successful management of knowledge since, in today's world, information has become a valuable resource and so have the people who understand and manage it. No longer can we think of information as a concrete entity. Instead, information is a restless friend, constantly changing. Increasingly society is turning to computers with greater power and ease of use, new information storage devices, and automated systems to deliver content or data. As a result we find our services evolving toward a "high tech" model as we encourage the use of technology to reduce manual processes and free the intellect for its proper function.

But our essential role remains the same: "connect people with the information they want, show them the possibilities and the routines."[5] Simply stated, we help people find resources by functioning as the living mind and human presence in this world of technology. Even in the midst of bytes and chips and floppy disks, these searchers still like the information provided in a very human and humane fashion. Just as society has increased its perception of the value of information, it is beginning to place a premium on service.

For reference librarians, this is surely cause for celebration. After all, we've been in the service business since Ashurbanipal founded his library at Nineveh. True, our concepts of service and who should receive it have progressed radically, but reference librarians have a long tradition to build on and a good record of success. For the most part, librarians enjoy the confidence of many satisfied seekers of truth (or at least the facts). Thus we have a unique opportunity to take a leadership role in helping to prepare society for the information age and ensuring access to information for all people in a caring way.

Librarians as a Central Mediating Force

Like everyone, academic libraries and their roles are changing. As knowledge increases in complexity, the organization of that knowledge is becoming more complicated and the physical media for storing and sorting data more diverse. The concepts surrounding the potential use of innovative technologies to access any kind of information located anywhere in the country or the world have excited both students and faculty. They are no longer content to spend hours in the library looking for documents that may or may not contain needed information. Instead these users have enthusiastically embraced automated systems for the delivery of content or the data and information contained in documents.

Consequently we are introducing onto the reference floor a variety of machines and technology designed to access vast quantities of information and librarians are assuming an active role as a central mediating force in the information explosion. As our users expand their access to a myriad sources, our role as intrepreters and information professionals is expanding since the gateway connecting people with the information they want is often a device that was just a gleam in someone's eye a year or two ago.

Perhaps nothing epitomizes this better than the very popular optical disk formats. Increasingly this technology is attracting users and extending reference tools to a wider audience. Its huge success stems in part from end-users' sense of unlimited access, ease of use and privacy, and the absence of time pressure. In addition, CD-ROMs are truly an end-user reference tool requiring virtually no instruction. Most students learn quickly on their own, take pride in teaching a friend, refuse to accept an alternative information source, and willingly stand around and wait for stations to become available for use.[6]

The introduction of CD-ROMs on the reference floor has given librarians an almost instant high-visibility stance as information professionals, capturing the imagination of students, faculty and administrators. This one piece of technology has provided librarians with an unique opportunity to open new doors by working more closely with students, becoming more involved in the instructional/learning process, and developing greater rapport with faculty members. Suddenly, the library is seen as a progressive place on the cutting edge of electronics, encouraging its users to take advantage of the novelty and sparkle of information technologies.

IMPACT OF TECHNOLOGY

And this is only the beginning. A variety of other products waits in the wings. Erasable optical disks, write-once read-many disks, "expert systems", and interactive compact disk systems show promise for students. As a result, many researchers predict an increased need for skilled information specialists to assist users with search strategies, interpretation of information, and selection of appropriate databases. While these automated systems may not necessarily relieve reference librarians of work, they are making it more effective. Because students want to use these systems, they ask more questions, listen more carefully to introductory comments, and request assistance when their searches go awry.

Obviously there are problems. The pace of change in information technologies is far faster than institutions and individuals can easily cope with. The changes are chaotic, with relatively little being truly standardized. The market place is offering more, newer, different products every day and buyers must purchase software/hardware often without careful study of the implications of becoming involved with one kind of technology or another. New and powerful search capacities organize, retrieve and manage information in perplexing systems not always user-friendly or error-forgiving. Publishing is expensive, fragmented, and specialized. Costs often outstrip budgeted funds. But with both students and faculty beginning to view the librarian as an accessible and essential information specialist, we have a tremendous opportunity to combine well-designed services incorporating traditional reference sources with the new technology and move beyond answering isolated reference questions into the role of assisting students and faculty to solve information problems.

Service is one of the most fundamental concepts in librarianship—especially to reference work. Margaret Stieg defines service as a "contribution to the wealth of others, as useful labor that does not necessarily produce a tangible commodity, and as a facility supplying a public demand."[7] While business and other entities are discovering the value of service, reference librarians for years have spelled out in their guidelines and standards a commitment to give the best possible assistance to each individual user of a library. And in our literature we have struggled and debated over the many questions revolving around the definitions and aspects of this service.

Recently we have begun to pay close attention to the user as an active participant rather than a passive consumer of information. Reference librarians now plan their activities around the assumption that every information seeker brings a distinct mindset to problem solving. They further recognize that people have their own information systems and cognitive styles that must interact with library systems designed for general use. In addition, these individuals are beginning to make value judgements about the quality of the service they receive. As John Guasperi states, "In the final analysis, perceived quality is the only quality that matters, since what the customer perceives is what the customer receives."[8] Thus successful libraries are centering their programs around a user-oriented climate and measuring their achievement in terms of the value of their service, access to a wide variety of information and technologies, and user satisfaction.

One of the great strengths of reference librarianship is this commitment to a set of humanistic values that puts a high premium on person-to-person relationships. Because of these values, reference service has remained a labor-intensive, helping profession. Thus it is possible for the reference department to incorporate high technology into its services while maintaining a caring attitude toward students and faculty alike. Indeed, "high tech", as noted above, often provides the staff with a means to infuse the information process with a sense of excitement. A review of the newsletters of the Library Orientation-Instruction Exchange (LOEX) Library Instruction Clearinghouse shows clearly how many ways creative librarians have found to meet their users' needs. Reference librarians everywhere are making something, sharing something and leaving something at work that wasn't there before. Whether designing a bibliography, procedure, manual, lesson plan, media presentation, new service or cooperative relationship, staffs recognize that their efforts are limited only by their attitudes and eagerness to reach out and speak to their users. They have sensed the change and responded with exactly the services that will best serve their public.

IMPACT ON SERVICE

As a number of authors have pointed out, there are a variety of dilemmas facing reference librarians. In the face of increasing demands for service we must recognize that our buildings, budgets and staffs are finite. New information resources are often very expensive to own and require librarians to constantly train and retrain if they are to stay abreast of database changes. The sheer bulk of materials, print and nonprint, published each year is daunting. The kinds of people seeking assistance at reference desks has changed presenting librarians often with users whose library experience consists of impatient chases after isolated pieces of data in near total ignorance of what library systems are all about. And there are the perennial questions about the structure of service points, manning levels, fees, evaluation, and training. However, with a solid concept of what service is and an openness to change, reference librarians can resolve many of these issues at the local level resulting in sensitive programs that meet the needs and expectations of their users.

CONCLUSION

Finally, we have a unique opportunity to take a leadership role in helping to design library services centered on developing information awareness and instilling the practices of information finding and lifelong learning. We must ensure that reference service in the twenty-first century remains a helping profession and services are delivered with a caring attitude. Although the promise of the new technologies and the predictions of futurists may not be realized completely as now projected, technological advancements have given and will continue to give more people access to more information than would have been imagined possible a generation ago. Greater accessibility to information, made possible by more complex systems for recording data, make it imperative that users be exposed to experiences that encourage the critical evaluation of information services and the information-seeking process itself. What an exciting time to be a reference librarian.

REFERENCES

1. Guthrie-Morse, Barbara. "The New Age." Community, Technical, and Junior College Journal 58 (December/January 1987-88): 30.
2. Sheridan, James J. "Teaching Thinking: Mission of the Humanities" Community, Technical and Junior College Journal 58 (August/September 1987): 19.
3. Sellers, Patricia. "What Customers Really Want." Fortune 121 (June 4, 1990): 58.

4. Swan, John. "Information and Madness." Library Journal 113 (February 1, 1988): 25.

5. Swan, p. 26.

6. Allen, Gillian. "Patron Response to Bibliographic Databases on CD-ROM." RQ 29 (Fall, 1989): 103-110; Jewell, Timothy. "CD-ROM and End-Users: The University of Washington Experience." CD-ROM Librarian 4 (January, 1989): 15-21.

7. Stieg, Margaret. "Technology and the Concept of Reference or What Will Happen to the Milkman's Cow?", Library Journal 115 (April 15, 1990): 46.

8. Drake, Miriam A. "Management of Information." College & Research Libraries 50 (September 1989): 527.

BIBLIOGRAPHY

Allen, Gillian. "Patron Response to Bibliographic Databases on CD-ROM." RQ 29 (Fall 1989): 103-110.

Bunge, Charles A. "Potential and Reality at the Reference Desk: Reflections on a "Return to the Field"." The Journal of Academic Librarianship 10 (July 1984): 128-133.

Drake, Miriam A. "Management of Information." College & Research Libraries 50 (September 1989): 521-531.

Ford, Barbara J. "Reference Service: Past, Present, and Future". College & Research Libraries News 49 (October 1988): 578-582.

Guthrie-Morse, Barbara. "The New Age." Community, Technical, and Junior College Journal 58 (December/January 1987-88): 30-32.

Jewell, Timothy. "CD-ROM and End-Users: The University of Washington Experience." CD-ROM Librarian 4 (January 1989): 15-21.

Martin, Susan K. "Information Technology and Libraries: Toward the Year 2000." College & Research Libraries 50 (July 1989): 397-405.

Miller, William and Bonnie Gratch. "Making Connections: Computerized Reference Services and People." Library Trends 37 (Spring 1989): 387-401.

Schultz, Kim and Kristine Saloman. "End Users Respond to CD-ROM." Library Journal 115 (February 1 1990): 56-57.

Sellers, Patricia. "What Customers Really Want." Fortune 121 (June 4 1990): 58-68.

Sheridan, James J. "Teaching Thinking: Mission of the Humanities." Community, Technical, and Junior College Journal 58 (August/September 1987): 18-21.

Stieg, Margaret F. "Technology and the Concept of Reference or What Will Happen to the Milkman's Cow." Library Journal 115 (April 15 1990): 45-49.

Swan, John. "Information and Madness." Library Journal 113 (February 1 1988): 25-28.

A Look Back at Twenty-Five Years Behind the Desk

Constance A. Fairchild

SUMMARY. This is an overview of my experiences in twenty-five years of working as a reference librarian in the University of Illinois Library at Urbana-Champaign. It includes a general discussion of reference librarianship, a description of my situation at Illinois, some changes that have occurred over the years, and some interesting aspects of the job. Included are a list of things that academic reference librarians should know, a discourse on the use of the computer in reference work, and a description of reference correspondence. There are two anecdotes; one an account of the "Salutation Army Band" and the other the case of the genealogist bikers.

The following comments are some of the observations and experiences that come to mind as I am about to complete my twenty-fifth year as a reference librarian at the University of Illinois at Urbana-Champaign. I would like to emphasize the interesting aspects of the work, as I have experienced it over the years. Some of the things that I did in the past are no longer part of the work of our department, and some aspects of the work have changed drastically. Anyone who has been in a profession for a long time can zero in on parts of the work that particularly appeal to him or her, so I would like to present here my own, possibly unorthodox, views on the subject of reference librarianship.

Any discussion of reference work should begin with a description of the attributes that one brings to the job, and the mindset that one develops after a number of years. I often think that everything I

Constance A. Fairchild is Assistant Reference Librarian, University of Illinois at Urbana-Champaign Library, 1408 W. Gregory, Urbana, IL 61801.

© 1991 by The Haworth Press, Inc. All rights reserved.

know eventually comes into play at the reference desk. Some would say that an inquiring mind is a necessity. I would say that idle curiosity is even more to the point. "Inquiring mind" implies a methodical acquiring of information. Idle curiosity implies a mind like a sponge, taking it all in and rejecting nothing as useless.

As reference librarians we must accept the fact that we spend most of our lives dispensing someone else's information. Unlike scholarly researchers who eventually get a proprietary corner on some esoteric aspect of the world of knowledge, we can make few claims for originality. In fact originality is discouraged since it is undocumented information. On the other hand, we take no responsibility for the flaws in someone else's scholarship. True talent lies in separating the good from the bad.

If I was asked to list the most valuable things an academic reference librarian should know, I should present a list that looks like this:

1. A phenomenal knowledge of geography, past and present, including locations of things, buildings, places, how they are spelled, where they fit in chronologically, and how they are related regionally.
2. A mental outline of world history, with as much detail as it is possible to absorb and retain. (Almost every reference question has to be oriented to some aspect of the two points listed above before it can begin to be answered. This becomes so automatic that one isn't usually aware that such an orientation is being made.)
3. A smattering of basic words in all the western languages, and some of the eastern ones, if possible.
4. An ability to use and interpret directories, bibliographies, etc. and to recognize the clues provided by such things as typography and the obscure abbreviations that can baffle all except the original compilers.
5. A mental cache of the names of prominent persons, past and present, the approximate dates when they lived, how their names are spelled, and a good familiarity with biographical sources, including those used by genealogists.

I should say something here about the benefits of genealogical research as a pursuit for reference librarians. Although genealogy is not an academically fashionable topic, and most people do it in their spare time, as I do, there are benefits. The most obvious is the practice it gives in pursuing a topic through a multitude of sources. Since genealogical sources vary widely in reliability, the real challenge is to separate the good information from the bad. Genealogy also provides a strong sense of historical continuity at the individual and family level. Family historians often find that popularly held assumptions about life in the past simply don't fit their own findings, and that the interpretations and analyses of professional historians are not of much practical use. I routinely extract only factual material from the sources I use, eliminating all the speculation about political, social and economic motives, unless it is directly related to the actions of the people I am studying. This is not to denigrate the work of scholars, but to emphasize the fact that interpretations become outdated, while documented facts retain their validity. One writer has said, "If you tell a story well enough, all the various theories and explanations become superfluous. The story is its own explanation."[1]

UNIVERSITY REFERENCE WORK

In *Civilisation* Lord Kenneth Clark stated, "I wonder if a single thought that has helped forward the human spirit has ever been conceived or written down in an enormous room: except, perhaps, in the reading room of the British Museum."[2] I hope the same exception could be made for the Reference Room at the University of Illinois Urbana-Champaign. Illinois alumnus Roger Ebert says, "As an undergraduate, I found the vast, high, light-filled reading room to be a sort of temple of learning—most of which I despaired of ever mastering—and in graduate school, after taking courses on the use of the library for research, I was even more awed by how much of human knowledge is contained in that building."[3] Certainly there is some psychological advantage in spending your working days in a room of cathedral proportions with an architectural ambiance worthy of Colonial Williamsburg. Aside from the obvious problems of climate control, which weren't even thought of in the 1920s when academic reading rooms and football stadiums were built with approximately the same square footage, the immense room causes its occupants to assume a sort of psychological cocoon enabling their many activities to go on simultaneously. People using the room pay little attention to anything except their own business. This may create problems if one feels obliged to interact with everyone who comes into the Reference Room. However I have always considered it an advantage for the independent-minded researcher who likes to work uninterrupted, and to request help when needed.

For the first twelve years that I worked in reference, I worked on interlibrary borrowing, a function that is no longer being done in our department. Searching of interlibrary loan requests, besides giving good experience in bibliographic verification, brings into play the smattering of foreign languages that I mentioned earlier. I developed such esoteric talents as knowing the vernacular name of every academy of sciences in Europe. I became intimately acquainted with the bibliographic details of a good many faculty and graduate research projects; although, to my frustration, I saw very few of the finished products. In particular, I remember one anthropology dissertation that was done on Polynesian quilts. I avidly read all the borrowed material before the graduate student ever saw it. I later read the dissertation, and it was fascinating.

THE EFFECTS OF THE COMPUTER

A few words should be said here about The Computer. The computer is the single biggest agent of change in reference work in the twenty-five years that I have been a reference librarian. In the early 1970s none of us had any clue that by 1980 our working lives would revolve around the idiosyncrasies of this box on the desk. Library computer systems and databases are essentially giant electronic data dumps, and it becomes a constant challenge to extract their secrets. Once you accept the fact that what you find in the computer today may not be there tomorrow, you find that your life is made easier, patrons are more satisfied, and slow times on the desk can be filled with bibliographic excursions through the systems catalogs. The hard-disk PC is an open invitation to creative effort in devising home-made data files, and several of my colleagues and I have tried our hands at doing this.

In 1985 I created a controlled vocabulary database of elusive, mainly local, information from our information card files and other sources, and set it up on the computer using a word processor and commercial software. Since it was intended for internal use in the department, I indulged my whims and added in biographies of local personalities, a few local myths, information about regional attractions, and some off-the-wall things like a list of the various sizes of wine and champagne bottles (you never know when someone will ask you for the number of ounces in a nebuchadnezzar). Members of my department gave me suggestions and additional information. In a situation like this one is limited only by one's imagination and the capacity of the hard disk. After a few years my database was incorporated into a larger system called "Illinois Search Aid" that was devised by another librarian. This enables us to do free text searching instead of using the controlled vocabulary, and makes it much easier to search. In-house data files are a lot of work to set up, but they are easier to maintain than paper files, and are a lot more fun to do.

In 1976 there occurred the first, and only, performance of the "Salutation Army Band", an event which was alluded to by Norman Stevens in one of his columns on library humor.[4] The full story of this can now be told.

I was approached several weeks before Christmas by one of the catalogers, who was proposing to form a band to play at the Catalog Department Christmas party, held annually in the cataloging room. She needed a bass drum, and she knew that my husband, who is a percussionist on the music faculty, could probably supply the item required. In addition to procuring the drum, I volunteered my services as a euphonium player. A somewhat motley band with rather unorthodox instrumentation was organized of members of the library staff, and we held one rehearsal in a fourth floor conference room. Our music consisted of Christmas carols photocopied from a hymn book. My colleague from the Catalog Department conducted the band and wrote a humorous program with a "biographical" sketch of each player. After serenading the party-goers we paraded through the second floor, playing at several choice spots, including the foyer outside the Reference Room. This proved to be one of the last great Catalog Department parties, as the concept of "holistic" librarianship took hold shortly thereafter, and the department was dispersed to other parts of the library.

"EASY RIDER" COMES TO THE REFERENCE DESK

In an academic reference department, we do not have a large number of questions from genealogists. When we do have such inquiries my colleagues and I do our best to steer the genealogists in the right direction. I must confess that my ultimate experience in this regard came the day that two rather hefty young men in bikers gear (jeans, boots and leather vests) came to the desk looking for books on heraldry. One had a typed family history obtained from a relative, and he wanted the family coat of arms. After studying the few books on heraldry that we keep in the Reference Room, they came back to the desk emptyhanded and explained that the coat of arms was needed to complete a tattoo; whereupon one of them pulled up his shirt and showed me the partially finished tattoo. After inspecting it I agreed that it was a fine tattoo, worthy of completion, and suggested some more possibilities of books in the bookstacks. I didn't see them again, but I hope they were successful.

One of the more interesting aspects of my job is something that I took on in 1989, and that is doing the correspondence for mail inquiries received from out-of-state. (In-state inquiries are handled elsewhere in the library). We receive about ten or twelve of these a month, and they come from all over the world. They generally have some tie-in with the University or the state of Illinois, although there are a few of the "send me all you have on . . . " variety. I have been pleasantly surprised by the care and detail put into many of the letters. I had thought that letter writing was becoming a lost art, and that I would be fielding a lot of vague requests. That apprehension has proved not to be the case. Maybe the letter is the last resort, when all else has failed. At any rate most writers are very specific about what they want, given the difficulties that they must have in visualizing just what can be obtained from us. One of the challenges of mail correspondence is in trying to gauge the sophistication and general situation of the writer, given nothing more than the clues in the letter. Do I explain interlibrary loan in detail, or do I just send the information expecting that the recipient will know what to do with it? If I guess wrong I will get a letter by return mail wanting me to mail out the book directly without benefit of intermediary.

CONCLUSION

In conclusion I would like to say that the rewards of reference librarianship lie in the intellectual challenges, and in the interactions with library users. Innovations in service can provide stimulation for users and librarians, but it is the day-to-day pursuit of information that keeps us alive intellectually and professionally.

REFERENCES

1. Shelby Foote, quoted in Tim Clark, "The man who had to kill Abraham Lincoln," *Yankee* 54 (October 1990): 82.
2. Lord Kenneth Clark, *Civilisation* (New York: Harper & Row, 1970), p. 192.
3. Roger Ebert, "Quotables," *Friendscript; Newsletter, University of Illinois Library Friends at Urbana-Champaign* 11 (Winter 1989-90): 7.
4. Norman D. Stevens, "Humor and creativity: Holidays," *C&RL News* 49 (November 1988): 675.

Librarians and Book Publication: Overcoming Barriers

Mary M. Nofsinger
Eileen E. Brady

SUMMARY. Academic librarians are under increasing pressure to publish due to universities' expectations for excellence in scholarly publication and research. Although much has been written on librarianship and professional development, very little addresses how reference librarians can pursue substantial writing and research projects in the face of other responsibilities. This article presents an overview of the book publication process, including initial planning, obtaining a contract with a publisher, legal considerations in regard to contracts, relationships with editors, doing the research, organizing the content, and preparing the manuscript. Publishing a book can be a rewarding personal and professional experience.

"Writing is a sweet and wonderful reward, but for what?"
— Franz Kafka

Many academic librarians are currently striving to meet their institution's expectations of scholarly publication for annual review, promotion and tenure.[1] Numerous articles and books document the professional disadvantages with which librarians contend in order to conduct research and publish the results,[2] difficulties largely due to the demands of other responsibilities including reference service. Furthermore, librarians who want or are compelled to do research are frequently left to their own devices in integrating this activity with other professional duties.[3] With little time to conduct research

---

Mary M. Nofsinger is Head of Reference, Humanities/Social Sciences, Holland Library, Washington State University, Pullman, WA 99164-5610. Eileen E. Brady is Head, Science Interlibrary Loan and USDA Document Delivery Service, Owen Science and Engineering Library, Washington State University, Pullman, WA 99164-3200.

© 1991 by The Haworth Press, Inc. All rights reserved.

within the requirements of their primary assignments, most reference librarians do not attempt to publish a book. Yet most university administrators place a high value on substantial scholarly works.

A librarian who has never written a book may not fully realize the numerous benefits from undertaking such a project. First, the research preceding the writing broadens a librarian's knowledge and understanding of a subject area, and thus improves that person's ability to provide specialized, in-depth reference service to users. Secondly, research findings contribute to the general knowledge base utilized by other library users. Third, writing and publication are excellent ways to achieve distinction. Alley, for example, discusses varied reasons for writing including professional recognition, career advancement, and promotion and tenure requirements.[4] Fourth, a librarian frequently becomes more aware of the problems facing scholars and develops a better understanding of the research process and the needs of teaching faculty.[5] Finally, a librarian author may derive considerable satisfaction from developing writing skills, meeting challenges, and achieving personal goals.

Reluctance to attempt publication of a monograph may be partly a consequence of the lack of concise information available to librarians on how to begin the long process of researching the topic, locating a publisher, writing the manuscript, and getting it published. However, the entire publication process will be more enjoyable if a librarian author has prior knowledge of the following tasks which can lead to a completed, publishable manuscript.

Since writing a book requires considerable time and effort, careful thought and preparation should occur prior to undertaking the project. During this preliminary interval, choosing a specific topic is the crucial task since it forces a prospective author to analyze the reasons for wanting to write the book. An individual librarian is often well qualified to recognize gaps in the literature and to address the needs of frustrated users pursuing elusive information. After performing a thorough literature search, the prospective author must analyze the viability of publishing a book on a particular topic: What would be unique, distinctive, or innovative about the proposed work? Any topic which could fill a unique theoretical, methodological, or substantive gap in the academic literature would be a strong possibility for publication. In addition, a librarian must ascertain whether or not he or she has the motivation and courage needed to follow through on a project which may take several years to complete.

Potential marketability is another key factor which a prospective author must investigate. An unwritten rule is "thou shalt not duplicate" publications currently available, since duplication of an existing work is one of the most common reasons why publishers reject proposals for new books.[6] If similar works exist, they must be reviewed and explicitly compared with the qualities of the proposed book.[7] Is there a sufficient quantity of new or previously undisclosed information available to justify another book-length publication? When assessing the potential market, a librarian should blend honesty and realism with a thorough analysis of the book's sales potential.

Finally, a prospective author needs to realistically estimate the time required to complete a manuscript for publication. Some librarians negotiate with administrators for small quantities of released time, although this has sometimes been found to be counterproductive due to faculty members' unproductive attitudes and poor work habits.[8] Another option to investigate is whether or not professional leave can be obtained for an extended time period. Since leave applications may take months to be approved, the reference librarian considering this option should contact publishers and submit an application for professional leave simultaneously. Probably the most realistic option for most librarians, however, is to write using available time during the regular year, i.e., working nights, weekends, and during vacations.[9] This requires a great deal of self-motivation, priority setting, self-discipline, and mutual understanding and support from family members.[10] Acknowledging that book writing is a time-consuming project reduces personal stress and makes the process more enjoyable.

LOCATING A PUBLISHER

How does a librarian author get one or more publishers in the appropriate subject field to seriously consider a proposal for a book? The next task is to compile a list of appropriate publishers to contact. Depending on the topic, the type of book planned, and the potential market, a prospective author could browse through listings in the *Publishers Trade List Annual*, talk with knowledgeable colleagues about the reputations of various publishers, examine recent books on the same topic, and talk to publishers' representatives at professional meetings regarding marketing plans, sales methods, and other matters. After selecting approximately ten potential publishers, the *Literary Market Place* should be consulted to obtain the names of specific editors to be contacted with the book proposal. One effective approach is to obtain permission from experienced authors to use their names in the initial approach to the editors identified. Van Til succinctly sums up the situation:

> The more attention a manuscript receives, the more likely it is to be published. Materials submitted by an author who has had no prior contact with the [publishing] house . . . have less than one in a hundred chances of getting published. In contrast, projects which come in as a result of an editor's efforts or connections . . . have a chance of about one in three of being published.[11]

Knowing these odds, prospective authors must carefully research and prepare a book proposal or *prospectus* which presents the nature, scope, and purpose of the manuscript. According to Mullins, "Most publishers are businessmen, not academicians. They may use your prospectus to evaluate not only your manuscript but also your ability to think, write, and do business."[12] Therefore, a librarian author should spend considerable time and effort preparing a prospectus which includes the following:

1. A brief description of the prospective work, the rationale for writing it, any bias or limitations toward the topic, and outstanding or unique features.
2. A statement of the intended primary and secondary markets which could include libraries, the general public, professional audiences, college students, etc. and the size of each estimated market.
3. A description of published books which are similar and an indication of their strengths and weaknesses. Point out unique substantive, methodological, theoretical, or pedagogical features of the proposed book.
4. An indication of the planned length and any special features

of the manuscript (such as illustrations, tables, etc.), the percentage which has been completed, and an estimated completion date.
5. A detailed outline of contents with headings and sub-headings. If possible, include a brief description of each chapter.
6. Samples of two or three consecutive chapters to show writing style and some of the manuscript's content.
7. A cover (query) letter to a specific editor which explains why that publishing house was chosen, why the book is needed, and what the author's qualifications are for writing it. A copy of the author's vita or resume listing degrees and previous publications could be included.
8. A stamped, self-addressed return envelope, which will identify the author as a knowledgeable professional who expects a prompt response to the book proposal.

After receiving the prospectus, the publisher's editorial review process may take two to three months or longer due to prior work schedules. If the editors and marketing specialists determine that the proposed book has strong market potential, the librarian author will probably receive a contract. As soon as contract negotiations have been concluded, the author must immediately notify other publishers to whom a prospectus was also submitted.

The old adage, "Look before you leap," is especially appropriate when contracting for a book. An author cannot afford to sign any contract without reading it thoroughly and understanding it completely. In general, a book publishing contract specifies the legal responsibilities of both the author and publisher regarding many issues, including payment for the book, advances, other costs, copyright issues, standard clauses, subsequent editions, options for future work, and failure to deliver a satisfactory manuscript as specified. Since literary agents and lawyers are expensive, most authors may want to educate themselves on what standard contract provisions to expect, items which are negotiable (especially contingency clauses), and pitfalls to avoid. There are numerous excellent legal resources available[13] to guide authors in regard to specific details. Finding the right publisher and negotiating favorable terms increases the likelihood that the project will be rewarding for the librarian author.

LOCATING RESEARCH MATERIALS

When librarians decide to become authors, they often have a distinct advantage in that their educational background includes knowledge of subject-specific resources and their training facilitates the ability to locate information in other disciplines. Possessing these information skills, a librarian author frequently finds that the research phase is the most challenging and enjoyable part of writing a book. After becoming familiar with available local resources including catalogs of materials in other libraries, documents, subject bibliographies, and archival listings, an author may have to travel to other research institutions to personally examine materials which are not accessible through interlibrary loan or other means.

After identifying the directors or archivists in charge of research institutions and major collections containing appropriate resources, a librarian author should *always* send a personal letter in advance of the visit. It is preferable to ask the head of the libraries to contact designated institutions on the librarian's behalf, requesting access to collections and facilities or services offered to scholars. Since institutions have numerous restrictions (limited hours, reader passes for admission, pencil note-taking in rare book areas, no laptop computers, in-house usage only, etc.), a librarian author needs to know institutional research policies in advance to plan for efficient use of time. Written documentation of permission to use the collection allows an author to gain immediate access to materials needed and facilitates pleasant working relationships with colleagues who may assist in the research process.

WRITING THE MANUSCRIPT

Once a sufficient quantity of material has been collected, the librarian author should begin preparing the first complete draft, the hardest part of the book writing process.[14] An author can enhance manuscript preparation by establishing a private space where interruptions can be kept to a minimum and by following a rough outline or plan. An author must consciously make choices to provide time for writing and then establish procedures to insure that regular progress is made. Setting realistic daily and weekly goals is extremely important for morale. Establishing an achievable pace and *planning* for regular rewards (going to a movie, watching TV, taking vacations, etc.) after meeting goals helps avoid procrastination. Despite these preparations, the following corollaries to Murphy's Law are very applicable to the manuscript preparation process: "Nothing is as easy as it looks, and everything takes longer than you think it will."[15]

Extra time should be allocated at the beginning stages of manuscript preparation since the author must carefully define the format for the book, gather writing tools, establish procedures, and become familiar with software or perhaps even learn a new computer system. As the research progresses, the author continually makes other decisions affecting the scope, organization, and content of the manuscript. Editors must be contacted whenever necessary for specific information on content, footnotes, format, proofreading questions, corrections, indexing procedures, draft deadlines, and other details.

Successful progress also depends on selecting appropriate equipment to do the work. A computer with enough disk capacity to store the entire manuscript is a basic necessity. Access to a letter-quality or laser printer is also recommended by editors. In addition, a word processing package which can perform the functions needed (graphs, indexing, alphabetizing, spell-checking, etc.) is essential. As with all software, basic safety precautions should be observed: making back-up copies of all files, updating every time changes are made, keeping each chapter in a separate file, using the same software throughout the manuscript, keeping a uniform format throughout, and storing backup files in a physically separated location. This is essential for the author's peace of mind. In addition, increased computer expertise is often a side benefit of the manuscript preparation process.

During the final stages of manuscript preparation, the librarian author is at last able to distill the overall findings from the substantial quantity of research completed. Now the introductory chapter can be written (or rewritten) to summarize the scope and focus of the research. In addition, indexes covering the entire book should be compiled. These are often time-consuming because they may reveal numerous errors which must be corrected. Due to in-depth familiarity with the subject content and knowledge of how useful a good index is for reference assistance, a conscientious author will provide users with superior access to information via appropriate indexes. In summary, an excellent index is a fundamental requirement for a good reference book and provides personal satisfaction to the librarian author.

GETTING IT PUBLISHED

Throughout the entire process of writing a book, a key factor in successful publication is the author's relationship with the editor assigned by the publishing house. Even before the contract is signed, the editor and author must correspond, discuss and clarify issues, and agree on general procedures for developing the manuscript. In general, editors prefer to work with an author as early as possible, preferably during the "idea stage."[16] Although some editors provide authors with the title of a preferred style guide, such as *The Chicago Manual of Style*, and written guidelines for authors, a RASD survey in 1987 found that a large majority of publishers surveyed (73 percent) had standards for bibliographic entries, but only 53 percent had supplied guidelines to authors.[17] Requesting written guidelines early on can greatly facilitate the writing process.

Editorial relationships can be further enhanced if a librarian author carefully prepares the manuscript according to instructions and scrupulously proofreads for errors prior to submission. There is one perennial rule for authors: *accuracy, accuracy, accuracy*. An author should also examine the manuscript for grammar, organization, style, and clarity before submitting it to an editor. In addition, a conscientious author must assume an active role in the publication process. Deadlines for submitting different segments of the book are usually set by editors. There may be times, however, when authors themselves must monitor when the manuscript needs to be reviewed. Ultimately, the author is responsible for providing on schedule the material an editor needs so that publication is not delayed.

As the manuscript moves through various stages of production (from initial drafts, to copy editing, to galley proofs, to page proofs or camera-ready copy, depending on publisher requirements), a series of editors will be consulting with the author. Throughout this process, the author should facilitate good relationships by maintaining regular contact with relevant editors at least once a month, by meeting publisher deadlines, and by treating editors in a professional, businesslike manner. In reality, the author and editor are partners, each striving to produce the best possible product, a finished manuscript. The author's ultimate reward will be prompt publication of the book and strong editorial support for future books.

When the book finally appears in print, the librarian author can finally relax and feel a sense of pride that a significant project has been completed. Although substantial amounts of time and energy have been invested in the publication process, the personal rewards are tremendous. The author may increase reference expertise in subject specific areas, develop a better understanding of users' needs and the research process, and strengthen his or her professional development in librarianship. In the final analysis, the librarian author's greatest satisfaction will come from successfully meeting personal goals and challenges.

REFERENCES

1. Robert Boice, Jordan M. Scepanski, and Wayne Wilson, "Librarians and Faculty Members: Coping with Pressures to Publish," *College & Research Libraries* 48 (November 1987): 494-503.

2. Fred Blatt, "Faculty Status for Academic Librarians: Justified or Just a Farce?" in *Issues in Librarianship: Views and Case Studies of the 1980s and 1990s*, eds. Peter Spyers-Duran and Thomas W. Mann, Jr. (Westport, Conn.: Greenwood Press, 1985), 115-128; Darrell L. Jenkins, M. Kathleen Cook, and Mary Anne Fox, "Research Development of Academic Librarians: One University's Approach," *The Journal of Academic Librarianship* 7 (May 1981): 83-86.

3. Jenkins, Cook, and Fox, "Research Development of Academic Librarians," 84.

4. Brian Alley and Jennifer Cargill, *Librarian in Search of a Publisher: How to Get Published* (Phoenix, Ariz.: Oryx Press, 1986), 6-7.

5. Stephen K. Sloan, "Research and Library Skills: An Analysis and Interpretation," *College & Research Libraries* 45 (March 1984): 99-109.

6. David M. Pilachowski and Noelene P. Martin, "How Do Bibliographies Get Published? A Survey of Publishers of Monographic Bibliographies," *RQ* 27 (Summer 1988): 542-546.

7. American Library Association, Reference and Adult Services Division (RASD), "Guidelines for the Preparation of a Bibliography," *RQ* 22 (Fall 1982): 31-32.

8. Robert Boice, "Is Released Time an Effective Component of Faculty Development Programs?" *Research in Higher Education* 26 (1987): 311-326.

9. William Van Til, *Writing for Professional Publication*, 2d ed. (Newton, Mass.: Allyn and Bacon, 1986), 152-54.

10. Ibid., 154.

11. Ibid., 147.

12. Carolyn J. Mullins, *A Guide to Writing and Publishing in the Social and Behavioral Sciences* (New York: John Wiley & Sons, 1977), 339.

13. Some reliable sources are Kirk Polking, ed., *Writer's Legal Guide* (Cincinnati, Ohio: Writers Digest Books, 1989); Mullins, *A Guide to Writing and Publishing*, 353-378; Tad Crawford, *The Writer's Legal Guide* (New York: Hawthorn Books, 1977).

14. Mullins, *A Guide to Writing and Publishing*, 50.

15. Anonymous, "Corollaries to Murphy's Law," *The Reader* (Chicago's Free Weekly) 5 (May 28, 1976): 2.

16. Pilachowski and Martin, "How Do Bibliographies Get Published?" 543.

17. Ibid., 544.

II. TOOLS OF THE PROFESSION

Ranking the Reference Books: Methodologies for Identifying "Key" Reference Sources

Richard L. Hopkins

SUMMARY. Limitations on both time and human memory make it impossible for the reference librarian or staff member to become aware of even a fraction of all the reference sources that have been published. There is, however, a small number of basic, fundamental or "key" sources that are widely used or widely recommended. In all likelihood these sources will answer a high proportion of all the questions that may appropriately be answered by published reference materials. This paper explores a number of ways that these "key" reference sources may be identified. The author concludes that a knowledge of the types or categories of reference materials that exist and what each type will do best, along with a knowledge of a corpus of basic, fundamental or "key" reference titles, will contribute to a firm foundation for effective and efficient reference service.

There are at least three good reasons why reference librarians should be interested in knowing what the most widely used, the

---

Richard L. Hopkins is Assistant Professor, School of Library, Archival and Information Studies, University of British Columbia.

© 1991 by The Haworth Press, Inc. All rights reserved.

most important, the "key" reference sources are. The first reason is simply the satisfaction of human curiosity, for surely one of the main purposes of reference librarianship, and one of its greatest pleasures, involves locating information that will answer questions that were motivated by someone's curiosity. It is the type of satisfaction we derive, for example, from learning that the ten most cited authors in the *Arts & Humanities Citation Index* for the period from 1976 to 1983 were Karl Marx (11,000 citations), Lenin (8,902), Shakespeare (8,060), Aristotle (7,745), the authors of the Bible as a group (7,035), Plato (6,904), Freud (6,111), Noam Chomsky (4,444), Hegel (4,439), and Cicero (4,386).[1]

The second reason for wanting to know what the "key" reference sources are might be termed "reference literacy." There are certain sources that *every* reference librarian needs to know, or at least to know about, if they are to be considered library literate. These terms and concepts relating to literacy, of course, are merely an extension to a specialized area of knowledge of the more general ideas developed by E.D. Hirsch Jr. in *Cultural Literacy: What Every American Needs to Know* and Hirsch, Kett and Trefil in *The Dictionary of Cultural Literacy*.[2]

The third reason for gaining a knowledge of key reference sources is a more pragmatic one. It is a reason that is both of interest and of significance to reference educators and to reference librarians charged with in-service training alike. Reference staff, both professionals and support staff, need to have a firm grasp and understanding of a basic corpus of reference materials. The main reason for this is obvious: the person working on the reference desk simply cannot afford the time to "reinvent the wheel" every time a patron asks a question. A set of routines, involving a knowledge of the reference interview, search strategies, and reference sources, must be stored in the memory in order to allow the reference worker to respond to reference questions in both an effective and an efficient manner.

Library science students, however, often complain that there are just too many reference sources to learn, and that besides every library is different and will therefore utilize a unique set of reference materials. The answer to the second part of this complaint is relatively straightforward. Even though every library has a unique clientele, and therefore perhaps a unique set of information needs and reference materials, every library also at one time or another has to go beyond the limits of its own resources in order to supply answers to questions. If the reference staff doesn't know of the existence of materials, even basic materials, other than those in its own collection, then accurate referral or interlibrary reference service becomes difficult if not impossible. Even for practical purposes, then, students will need to learn about some reference sources that they will never actually directly use themselves.

The answer to the first part of the complaint is somewhat more difficult to provide, for it is true indeed that there are too many reference sources to learn in any meaningful way. One of the first problems that the reference teacher faces, in fact, is to determine which reference sources merit attention at an introductory level out of the literally thousands of sources that have been published. Admittedly many sources, particularly those associated with a specific subject area, can be deferred to senior level courses, but that still leaves thousands of other titles to choose from. Restrictions on classroom time and human limits to the amount of information that can profitably be assimilated in a relatively short period of time, both dictate that these many sources be reduced to a manageable number.

Fortunately significant economies of effort can be achieved by focusing on the most widely used, the most important, the "key" reference sources. Bradford's Law of Scattering, an important bibliometric law, has important insights to offer here. Bradford "found that a small number of journals in a field yielded a high proportion of all the relevant articles."[3] It does not take a great leap of the imagination to project that for those reference questions that are most appropriately answered by published reference sources, a relatively small number of sources will answer a high proportion of all the questions asked (although the present author has not yet seen any empirical evidence to substantiate this).[4] This implies that the most widely used or most important general reference sources be identified at the outset of any introductory reference course. By identifying and then concentrating on two or three hundred important or "key" reference sources the reference instructor will be providing his/her students with a basic corpus of knowledge that will supply answers for the majority of reference questions, and will thereby be providing them with a solid foundation for offering both effective and efficient reference service.

The difficulty, of course, lies in deciding which reference sources are "key" sources, that is, those that are widely used or are widely regarded to be important sources. In all likelihood it is not possible to arrive at a definitive answer to this question, that is, it is not possible to compile a completely definitive list of basic reference sources. To achieve this, too many different types of data would need to be gathered and combined: for example, sales statistics, a survey of librarians in all types of libraries as to which sources they use to answer questions or which sources they consider to be important, a survey of library school instructors as to which sources they teach in basic courses, bibliometric studies of use of reference sources by scientists and scholars, etc.

DEFINITIVE ANSWER

The fact that a definitive answer may not be possible, of course, does not preclude attempts to arrive at answers that are less complete. Larsen, in fact, made one such attempt in 1978 when he surveyed sixty-three ALA-accredited library education programs. Faculty members responsible for teaching basic reference courses "were asked to submit syllabi or lists of the specific titles presented in their reference courses."[5] Larsen received responses from thirty-one accredited schools.

It was Larsen's survey, in fact, that stimulated an interest in one of the author's students, Arthur Coren, in a course on the literature of the arts and humanities, to explore the question of which reference books were the most widely recommended or used. The present author had devised an assignment for the course that utilized both published guides and citation indexes that would help to reveal to students the nature and structure of various subject areas in the literatures of the arts and humanities.[6] Each student in the course selected a subject area in the arts and humanities to study. Then, by examining introductory sources (guides to the literature, general encyclopedias, subject encyclopedias, handbooks, introductory monographs, etc.) the students compiled a list of recommended monographs in their field. These monographs were placed in rank order based on the number of recommendations they had received in the introductory sources. The top twenty titles were checked in all of the published volumes of the *Arts & Humanities Citation Index*. A second rank order list was then produced based on the number of citations each title had received. The final part of the assignment involved critically comparing the similarities and differences between the two lists.

Coren's first task in his assignment, entitled "Key Reference Titles: Who Uses Them?", was to identify published lists of recommended reference sources. Initially he identified three such lists or sets of lists: "Landmarks of Reference," a column appearing in *Reference Services Review* (RSR) over a four year period from October/December 1980 to Winter 1983 which yielded 9 sources; "Personal Choice" or "Desert Island" (name varies), a column appearing in *RSR* from the Fall 1982 issue to the Summer 1987 issue, which yielded 128 sources; and "*RQ* 25th Anniversary List of Distinguished References," published in the Fall 1985 issue of *RQ*, which yielded 25 sources.

When these three lists or sets of lists were combined, only 14 sources had been mentioned by three or more commentators. These sources are listed here in rank order along with the number of times they were each recommended:

Times Atlas of the World (7)	Encyclopedia of World Art (4)
World Almanac and Book of Facts (6)	McGraw-Hill Encyclopedia of Science and Technology (4)
The Bible (5)	New Encyclopedia Britannica (4)
Familiar Quotations (5)	United States Government Manual (3)
New Grove Dictionary of Music and Musicians (5)	Webster's Third New International Dictionary (3)
Oxford English Dictionary (5)	Whitaker's Almanac (3)
Encyclopedia of Bioethics (4)	World Book Encyclopedia (3)

These results are interesting, but are very limited both in terms of numbers and in terms of accuracy. The present author suspects, for example, that the relatively high positions accorded to the *Times Atlas of the World* and to *The Bible* in this list of reference sources are a result of the basic premise behind the "Personal Choice/Desert Island" column, namely selecting sources to use while "stranded on a desert island" (all of the choices for these two sources did in fact come from this column).

A more satisfactory list, both in terms of number of sources and representativeness, Coren found, was the one derived from the results of Larsen's survey. This holds true even despite the fact that Larsen did not find as much agreement amongst the reference teachers about what reference sources were considered to be basic as he had anticipated. Larsen found that there were 2,014 titles when all of the sources from all thirty-one of the schools were combined, but that "only 7.3 percent of the total number are agreed upon by half or more of the schools,"[7] that is, only 147 titles were taught by 16 or more of the schools. Extending Larsen's analysis further, it was found that only 70 titles, or roughly 3.5% of the total, were taught by 23 or more of the schools (about 75% of the schools involved), and that only 20 titles, or roughly 1% of the total, were taught by 28 or more schools (about 90% of the schools). Only 7 titles were taught by all 31 of the schools: *Current Biography*, *Dictionary of American Biography*, *Encyclopedia Britannica*, *New York Times Index*, *Reader's Guide to Periodical Literature*, *World Almanac and Book of Facts*, and *World Book Encyclopedia*. Clearly, experts in the field were far from unanimous, except for a very small number of titles, on what reference titles are considered to be basic or fundamental (the 70 sources taught by 75% or more of the schools in the study are listed in rank order in Appendix A).

Coren, finally, turned to citation counting as one further type of evidence for establishing the wide use or importance of selected reference sources. In doing so he encountered a number of problems. The first of these involved selecting a representative and yet manageable list of reference sources that could be checked in the three basic citation indexes, *Science Citation Index* (SCI), *Social Sciences Citation Index* (SSCI), and *Arts & Humanities Citation Index* (AHCI).[8] It would not have been possible, given the limitations of manual searching that Coren faced, to search more than a limited number of sources in these three indexes. A representative and manageable list of twenty sources was achieved by combining the results of Larsen's survey with the results achieved by combining the three lists or sets of lists published in the reference periodicals.

A further problem that was encountered with the citation search was a result of the lack of authority control in the citation indexes. Care had to be taken that all of the variant entries for each title were counted in order to ensure a reasonable degree of accuracy.

The most serious problem with utilizing citation data to rate the importance of reference sources, however, appeared in the analysis stage. It became clear that some reference sources were cited more than others not only because of their relative importance, but also because of the nature of their content. Reference books are more likely to be cited if they need to be referred to as a documented authority for some fact or statistic (e.g.: *Statistical Abstract of the United States*, etc.) or if they are substantive in nature (e.g.: *New Encyclopedia Britannica*, etc.). Reference books are less likely to be cited if they are referred to for factual information that does not have to be documented or if they are not substantive in nature (e.g.: *Encyclopedia of Associations, Acronyms, Initialisms and Abbreviations Dictionary*, etc.). The four citation ranking lists produced by Coren, one for *SCI*, one for *SSCI*, one for *AHCI*, and a combined list, are nevertheless interesting in their own right, and are reproduced as Appendixes B to E.

GENERATING A BASIC LIST

After examining Coren's study, the present author decided to extend the work in this area by attempting yet another approach to generating a basic list of widely used or important reference sources. He chose as the basis for his study four well-established textbooks that were designed for the teaching of basic or fundamental reference sources. These are in order of publication date:

Cheney, Frances Neel and Williams, Wiley J. *Fundamental Reference Sources*. 2nd ed. Chicago: American Library Association, 1980.

Hede, Agnes Ann. *Reference Readiness: A Manual for Librarians and Students*. 3rd ed. Hamden, Conn.: Library Professional Publications, 1984.

Taylor, Margaret T. and Powell, Ronald R. *Basic Reference Sources: A Self-Study Manual*. 3rd ed. Metuchen, N.J.: Scarecrow Press, 1985.

Katz, William A. *Introduction to Reference Work: Volume 1: Basic Information Sources*. 5th ed. New York: McGraw-Hill, 1987.

These four textbooks were aimed at slightly different audiences but they did nevertheless all clearly attempt to present what the authors considered to be "basic" or "fundamental" reference sources. The assumption underlying the present study was a relatively simple one: the greater the number of textbooks that listed a reference source the more fundamental or important the source was. If a reference source was listed by all four textbooks then it was considered to be more basic or important than one listed in only three texts.

The author compared the entries in the four texts by starting with the textbook that appeared to list the fewest sources (Hede) and then checked the entries in the other three texts. Once Hede was completed the author then checked the entries in the text next in terms of number of sources (Taylor and Powell) with the listings in Cheney and Williams and Katz. This methodology did not permit an accurate count of the total number of unique titles presented in all four textbooks, but this total may be fairly accurately estimated. Counting the number of sources listed in the index of Cheney and Williams, the text with the greatest number of sources, provided a total of 891 titles. Then, counting the number of titles beginning with the letter "A" in Cheney and Williams provided a total of 81 sources. Finally, counting the number of additional unique titles beginning with the letter "A" in Hede, Taylor and Powell and Katz, provided totals of 8, 11 and 24 respectively. These 43 titles represented an increase of about 53% over the 81 titles listed in Cheney and Williams. If the grand total in Cheney and Williams is multiplied by

53% this would provide an additional 472 titles to be added to the grand total (891 × 53% = 472 titles). Adding the two totals, one arrives at a final total of 1363 unique titles. One can be fairly confident, then, in saying that the four textbooks taken together list between 1300 and 1400 unique reference titles. For the sake of convenience the arbitrary figure of 1350 sources will be used for the calculations that follow.

When all of the sources had been tabulated it was found that the four texts had listed only 81 sources in common, or about 6% of the total (in Larsen's study all 31 schools could only agree on 7 sources out of 2014, less than 1% of the total). At least three texts in the present study agreed on an additional 132 sources, for an additional 10% of the total. Adding the two together, it was found that three or more of the textbooks had agreed upon 213 out of a total of 1350 sources, or about 16% of the total (in Larsen's study 75% or more of the schools had agreed upon 70 out of a total of 2014 sources, or about 3.5% of the total).

Bill Katz has asserted, in the preface to his textbook, that "there is no consensus on what constitutes 'basic'" reference titles.[9] This statement can be modified somewhat now to the more accurate observation that there appears to be an inverse relationship between consensus on basic reference titles and the number of experts or commentators involved. The greater the number of experts or commentators involved in the selection process the less agreement there is on what constitutes a corpus of basic or fundamental reference sources. One can only speculate about the reasons for this finding. First, it seems likely that every reference expert or commentator will have had a unique background of experience in reference work. Every reference title will, therefore, have had a different emphasis or importance in every commentator's previous work experience. A second factor could be that local needs or conditions will tend to increase the importance of some reference titles and will tend to diminish the importance of others.

Whatever the reasons for the fairly limited consensus, the fact is that there was more agreement amongst the four textbook commentators (all agreed on 6% of the sources, and at least 3 out of 4 agreed on 16% of the sources) than amongst the thirty-one library school instructors (all agreed on less than 1% of the sources, while 3 out of

4 agreed on 3.5% of the sources). Similar to Larsen, however, the present author expected to find an even greater degree of agreement amongst the experts in his study than he actually found. Aside from the factors discussed above, two other factors might be used to help account for the relatively low level of agreement amongst the textbook authors. The first is the fact that the texts are clearly aimed at slightly different audiences. Hede, for example, appears to place more emphasis on children's reference sources and on school library sources than the other texts; Taylor and Powell's text is designed for self-study; Cheney and Williams' text does not attempt to cover all types of reference sources; Katz observes that not "all so-called basic titles are included," because, among other reasons, "the objective of this text is to discuss various forms, and the titles used are those which best illustrate those forms."[10] A second factor that should be noted here is that the textbooks range in publication date from 1980 to 1987 and so newer reference titles by necessity will be somewhat underrepresented.

NEGATIVE TO THE POSITIVE

The view taken in this study, however, is that if all of these factors (different work experience of commentators, different intended audiences, and different publication dates) do indeed produce less agreement about what reference sources can be considered to be basic or fundamental, then this should be considered a positive rather than a negative outcome of the process. This is so because each source included on the final list may then be truly considered to be a basic, fundamental or "key" reference source, having withstood both the test of four independent judgments and the test of time.

The author has listed the results of the textbook study in Appendix F.[11] The reference sources have been classified and arranged in alphabetical order by type of source. Within each type those recommended by all four textbooks are listed first, followed by those sources listed by only three textbooks. Although classifying sources into groups by type may lead to some disagreement about where an individual source should be placed (is the *Statistical Abstract of the United States* a handbook or is it a yearbook?), this arrangement was thought to be the best one for allowing readers to make useful comparisons.

Larsen, in his study, made some attempt to summarize his results in terms of the number of titles in each category by type of reference source. Taking all 2014 titles he found that "There were 370 bibliographical information sources listed by at least one library school. The next largest categories were handbooks and indexes with 351 and 246 titles, respectively."[12] Examining just those sources listed in his study by 23 or more schools (75% of the schools) the following approximate percentages for each category, listed in rank order, result: biographical sources (20%); indexes (16%); dictionaries (14%); bibliographies (10%); encyclopedias (10%); handbooks (7%); yearbooks (7%); geographical sources (6%); serial reference sources (6%); government publication reference sources (3%); directories (1%). The results of the present study for those sources listed by 3 or more textbooks (75% of the textbooks), provide the following approximate percentages for each category in rank order (the categories differ somewhat from those used by Larsen): bibliographies (24%); indexes/abstracts (14%); dictionaries (12%); biographical sources (12%); encyclopedias (10%); yearbooks (9%); geographical sources (5%); guides (5%); library/book trade journals (4%); handbooks (3%); directories (1%); and news services (1%).

Another comparison that can be made with Larsen's study is to note any discrepancies between the sources listed in the two studies. First, Larsen's list of 70 sources taught by 75% or more of the schools can be compared with the 213 sources listed by 75% or more of the textbooks. When this comparison is carried out there are five titles on Larsen's list that do not appear on the textbook list: *The Lincoln Library of Essential Information* (listed by only 2 texts); *Funk & Wagnall's New Standard Dictionary of the English Language* (listed by 2 texts); *Directory of American Scholars* (listed by 2 texts); *Reader's Encyclopedia* (listed by 1 text); and *World Bibliography of Bibliographies* (listed by 2 texts). The author feels that the discrepancies here can most likely be explained by the fact that the information in these five sources has become dated over time and is therefore no longer current enough to be widely recommended.

Next, the 81 titles that were included in all four textbooks can be compared with the 142 sources that were listed in Larsen's study by 50% or more of the library schools. When this comparison is carried out it is discovered that there are 17 titles on the textbook list that do not appear on Larsen's list. Four of these titles can be accounted for by the fact that they were published only a few years before Larsen's study in 1978: *6,000 Words* (1976), *Webster's Collegiate Thesaurus* (1976), *Encyclopedia Buying Guide* (1976), and *Introduction to U.S. Public Documents* (1975). Several other titles were first published in the mid-to-late 1960s: *Children's Books in Print* (1969), *Subject Guide to Forthcoming Books* (1967), *Random House College Dictionary* (1968), *Merit Student's Encyclopedia* (1967), *Reader's Digest Almanac and Yearbook* (1966; an interesting question to research here would be how long it takes a reference source to become well established, especially in the relatively conservative guides to reference sources and in introductory textbooks). Five other titles, however, had been published for some considerable time: *Library of Congress Catalogs: Subject Catalog* (1950-), *Concise Oxford Dictionary of Current English* (1911-), *Webster's New World Dictionary of English Language* (1953-), *Publishers Weekly* (1872-), and *Occupational Outlook Handbook* (1949-). The only explanation for the absence of these sources from Larsen's list that makes sense is that they must have been taught and listed by fewer than half of the schools in his study. Why reference sources that have been listed by all four introductory reference textbooks, however, should be taught by less than half of the library schools surveyed must remain a puzzle.

Larsen, finally, concluded from his study that the tabulation of "titles currently agreed upon by reference instructors at ALA-accredited library education programs," could be useful to individual reference instructors when it came time to assess the sources they presented in basic reference courses.[13] The present author feels that the lists he has produced can be of use to both library school reference teachers and to reference librarians charged with the responsibility of in-service training of staff. He certainly, however, given the current pedagogical understandings in reference teaching, does not advocate having students learn these sources by rote memory. Instead, reference sources should be taught using the broader framework of types or categories of sources, with emphasis on what each type or category can do best, on strengths and weaknesses, etc. As Bill Katz has expressed it, "the objective . . . is to discuss various forms" of reference sources, "and the titles used are those which best illustrate those forms."[14] The present author would argue, however, that among those titles used to best illustrate different forms or types of reference materials, serious consideration should be given to utilizing those reference sources that both continue to be widely recommended and that have stood the test of time.

REFERENCES

1. Eugene Garfield, "Current Comments: The 250 Most-Cited Authors in the *Arts & Humanities Citation Index*, 1976-1983," *Current Contents* 48:3-10 (Dec. 1, 1986).
2. E.D. Hirsch, Jr., *Cultural Literacy: What Every American Needs to Know* (Boston: Houghton, 1987) and E.D. Hirsch, Jr., Joseph F. Kett and James Trefil, *The Dictionary of Cultural Literacy* (Boston: Houghton, 1988); see also Charles A. D'Aniello, "Cultural Literacy and Reference Service," *RQ* 28:370-80 (Spring 1989).
3. The *ALA Glossary of Library and Information Science*, s.v. "Bradford's Law of Scattering."
4. A news note reprinted in *The Unabashed Librarian* relates how "Dr. Herbert Goldhor at the recent LIBRARIES ON THE MOVE meeting suggested seven basic reference books that all libraries should have. They are: *World Almanac, Information Please Almanac, World Book Encyclopedia, Stevenson's Book of Quotations, An Unabridged Dictionary, A Motors Auto Repair or Chilton's Manual, Readers' Guide*". Dr. Goldhor, presumably with tongue firmly planted in cheek, said "that over 80% of reference questions could be answered by these basic tools." *The Unabashed Librarian* 59 (1986):24.
5. John C. Larsen, "Information Sources Currently Studied in General Reference Courses," in Bill Katz and Anne Clifford, eds., *Reference and Information Services: A New Reader*, (Metuchen, N.J.: Scarecrow Press, 1982), p. 408; originally published in *RQ* 18:341-48 (Summer 1979).
6. Richard L. Hopkins, "Perspectives on Teaching Social Science and Humanities Literatures," *Journal of Education for Library and Information Science* 28:136-51 (Fall 1987).
7. Larsen, "Information Sources Currently Studied in General Reference Courses," p. 409.

8. Coren searched *SCI* for the period from January 1980 to April 1987, *SSCI* for the period from January 1976 to August 1987, and *AHCI* for the period from January 1980 to August 1987.

9. William A. Katz, "Preface," *Introduction to Reference Work: Volume 1: Basic Information Sources*, 5th ed. (New York: McGraw-Hill, 1987), p. xii.

10. Ibid.

11. Change, it appears, is the only constant with reference books and reference publishing. For example, *Ayer Directory of Publications* is now *Gale Directory of Publications*; *Irregular Serials and Annuals* is now part of *Ulrich's International Periodicals Directory*; *Ulrich's Quarterly* is now *Bowker International Serials Database Update*; *Subject Guide to Forthcoming Books* is now part of *Forthcoming Books*; *Who's Who in Library and Information Science* has now been superseded by *Directory of Library and Information Professionals*; *6,000 Words* has been superseded by *12,000 Words*; *Encyclopedia Buying Guide* has been superseded by *Best Encyclopedias*; *Reference and Subscription Books Reviews* is now *Reference Books Bulletin*; and *Keesing's Contemporary Archives* is now *Keesing's Record of World Events*.

12. Larsen, "Information Sources Currently Studied in General Reference Courses," p. 409.

13. Ibid., p. 416.

14. Katz, "Preface," p. xii.

APPENDIX A.
LIBRARY SCHOOL STUDY

Sources Reported by 31 Schools (in alphabetical order)

Current Biography

Dictionary of American Biography

New Encyclopedia Britannica

New York Times Index

Reader's Guide to Periodical Literature

World Almanac & Book of Facts

World Book Encyclopedia

Sources Reported by 30 Schools

Biography Index

Collier's Encylopedia

Statistical Abstract of the United States

Sources Reported by 29 Schools

Dictionary of National Biography

Encyclopedia Americana

Facts on File

New Columbia Encyclopedia

Oxford English Dictionary

Statesman's Yearbook

Webster's Biographical Dictionary

Who's Who in America

Sources Reported by 28 Schools

Book of Famous First Facts

Ulrich's International Periodicals Directory

Sources Reported by 27 Schools

Ayer Dictionary of Publications

Information Please Almanac

Public Affairs Information Service

Union List of Serials

Who Was Who in America

Sources Reported by 26 Schools

Bibliographic Index

Cumulative Book Index

Encyclopedia of Associations

Guiness Book of World Records

Library Literature

Lincoln Library of Essential Information

New Serials Titles

Poole's Index to Periodical Literature

Random House Dictionary of the English Language

Sources Reported by 25 Schools

Acronyms, Initialisms and Abbreviations Dictionary

Books in Print

Columbia Lippincott Gazetteer

Compton's Encyclopedia

Contemporary Authors

Dictionary of American English on Historical Principles

Essay & General Literature Index

Familiar Quotations

Funk & Wagnall's New Standard Dictionary of the English Language

International Who's Who

National Union Catalog

New Century Cyclopedia of Names

Official Congressional Directory

Publisher's Trade List Annual

Webster's Second New International Dictionary of the English Language

Sources Reported by 24 Schools

American Book Publishing Record

American Heritage Dictionary

Directory of American Scholars

U.S. Government Manual

U.S. Monthly Catalog

Webster's Third New International Dictionary of the English Language

Europa Yearbook
Granger's Index to Poetry
Reader's Encyclopedia

Whitaker's Almanac
Who's Who

Sources Reported by 23 Schools

American Men and Women
  of Science
Dictionary of Slang and
  Unconventional English
Historical Atlas
  (Shepherd)
Nineteenth Century
  Reader's Guide
Rand McNally Commercial
  Atlas

Subject Guide to Books
  In Print
Times Atlas of the
  World
Webster's New Dictionary
  of Synonyms
Weekly Record

World Bibliography
  of Bibliographies

APPENDIX B.
SCIENCE CITATION INDEX

Statistical Abstract of the United States	597 citations
Encyclopaedia Britannica	239
Oxford English Dictionary	91
Webster's Third New International Dictionary	83
World Almanac & Book of Facts	46
Dictionary of Scientific Biography	35
Times Atlas of the World	24
McGraw-Hill Encyclopedia of Science and Technology	21
Familiar Quotations	19
World Book Encyclopedia	16
Dictionary of American Biography	15
Whitaker's Almanack	14
Who's Who in America	5
Encyclopedia of Bioethics	3
Encyclopedia of Associations	2
U.S. Government Manual	2
Acronyms, Initialisms and Abbreviations Dictionary	1
New Grove Encyclopedia of Music and Musicians	1
Contemporary Authors	0
Reader's Encyclopedia	0

APPENDIX C.
SOCIAL SCIENCE CITATION INDEX

Webster's Third New International Dictionary	531 citations
Encyclopaedia Britannica	424
Statistical Abstract of the United States	424
Oxford English Dictionary	375
World Almanac & Book of Facts	165
Dictionary of American Biography	116
Familiar Quotations	73
Who's Who in America	73
Dictionary of Scientific Biography	55
U.S. Government Manual	27
World Book Encyclopedia	23
Encyclopedia of Associations	22
McGraw-Hill Encyclopedia of Science and Technology	21
Times Atlas of the World	21
Whitaker's Almanack	20
Encyclopedia of Bioethics	6
Reader's Encyclopedia	5
Contemporary Authors	4
Acronyms, Initialisms and Abbreviations Dictionary	2
New Grove Dictionary of Music and Musicians	2

APPENDIX D.
ARTS & HUMANITIES CITATION INDEX

Oxford English Dictionary	242 citations
Encyclopaedia Britannica	203
Dictionary of American Biography	110
Webster's Third New International Dictionary	73
New Grove Dictionary of Music and Musicians	59
Dictionary of Scientific Biography	39
Who's Who in America	25
Familiar Quotations	24
World Almanac & Book of Facts	23
Statistical Abstract of the United States	18
Reader's Encyclopedia	10
Contemporary Authors	9
Times Atlas of the World	5
McGraw-Hill Encyclopedia of Science and Technology	4

Encyclopedia of Associations	3
World Book Encyclopedia	3
Whitaker's Almanack	2
Acronyms, Initialisms and Abbreviations Dictionary	0
Encyclopedia of Bioethics	0
U.S. Government Manual	0

APPENDIX E.
SCI, SSCI AND AHCI COMBINED

Statistical Abstract of the United States	1039 citations
Encyclopaedia Britannica	866
Oxford English Dictionary	708
Webster's Third New International Dictionary	687
Dictionary of American Biography	241
World Almanac & Book of Facts	234
Dictionary of Scientific Biography	129
Familiar Quotations	116
Who's Who in America	103
New Grove Dictionary of Music and Musicians	62
Times Atlas of the World	50
McGraw-Hill Encyclopedia of Science and Technology	46
World Book Encyclopedia	42
Whitaker's Almanack	36
U.S. Government Manual	29
Encyclopedia of Associations	27
Reader's Encyclopedia	15
Contemporary Authors	13
Encyclopedia of Bioethics	9
Acronyms, Initialisms and Abbreviations Dictionary	3

APPENDIX F.
TEXTBOOK STUDY

Bibliographies Listed in Four Textbooks (in alphabetical order)

American Bibliography
(Evans)

American Book Publishing
Record

National Index of American
Imprints Through 1800 (Shipton & Mooney)
National Union Catalog

Ayer Directory of Publications
Bibliotheca Americana
  (Sabin)
Books in Print
Children's Books in Print
Cumulative Book Index

Forthcoming Books

Irregular Serials and Annuals
Library of Congress Catalogs:
  Subject Catalog
Monthly Catalog of United States
  Government Publications
Monthly Checklist of State
  Publications

New Serial Titles
Paperbound Books in Print

Publisher's Trade List Annual
Subject Guide to Books in Print
Subject Guide to Forthcoming
  Books in Print
Ulrich's International Periodicals
  Directory
Union List of Serials
United States Catalog: Books
  in Print
Vertical File Index

Weekly Record

Bibliography Listed in Three Textbooks

American Bibliography...
  1801-1819 (Shaw & Shoe-
  maker
American Catalogue of Books,
  1861-1871 (Kelly)
American Catalogue of Books,
  1876-1910
American Newspapers,
  1821-1936
Audiovisual Materials
  (Library of Congress)

Author-Title Index to
  Sabin's Dictionary (Molnar)
Bibliotheca Americana
  (Roorbach)
Comprehensive Dissertation
  Index
Dissertation Abstracts
  International

British Books in Print

British Library, General
  Catalogue of Printed Books
British National
  Bibliography
Bureau of the Census.
  Catalog of Publications
Checklist of American
  Imprints For 1820-1829
  (Shoemaker)
Checklist of American
  Imprints For 1830-
Children's Catalog

Newspapers in Microform

Public Library Catalog

Fiction Catalog

Guide to Microforms in Print

History and Bibliography
  of American Newspapers
Junior High School
  Library Catalog
Music: Books on Music
  and Sound Recordings
  (Library of Congress)

Senior High School
  Library Catalog
Standard Periodical
  Directory
Subject Guide to Children's
  Books in Print
Ulrich's Quarterly

Biographical Sources Listed in Four Textbooks

Biography Index

Chamber's Biographical
  Dictionary
Current Biography Yearbook

Dictionary of American
  Biography

Dictionary of National
  Biography
New Century Cyclopedia
  of Names
Webster's Biographical
  Dictionary
Who's Who in America

Biographical Sources Listed in Three Textbooks

American Men and Women
  of Science
Biography & Genealogy
  Master Index
Contemporary Authors

International Who's Who

New York Times
  Biographical Service
New York Times
  Obituaries Index
Twentieth Century Authors

Who's Who

Who's Who Among
  Black Americans
Who's Who in American
  Art
Who's Who in American
  Politics
Who's Who in Library
  and Information Science
Who's Who in the World

Who's Who of American
  Women

Webster's American
   Biographies
Who Was Who in America

World Authors, 1950-1970

Dictionaries/Wordbooks Listed in Four Textbooks

Acronyms, Initialisms and
   Abbreviations Dictionary
American Heritage
   Dictionary
Concise Oxford Dictionary
   of Current English
Dictionary of American
   Slang
Dictionary of Modern
   English Usage
Dictionary of Slang and
   Unconventional English
Oxford English Dictionary

Random House College
   Dictionary

Random House Dictionary
   of the English Language
Roget's International
   Thesaurus
6,000 Words

Webster's Collegiate
   Thesaurus
Webster's New Dictionary
   of Synonyms
Webster's New World Dictionary
   of the English Language
Webster's Second New
   International Dictionary of the
   English Language
Webster's Third New
   International Dictionary of the
   English Language

Dictionaries/Wordbooks Listed in Three Textbooks

Abbreviations Dictionary
American Heritage School
   Dictionary
Dictionary of American English
   on Historical Principles
Dictionary of Americanisms on
   Historical Principles
Harper Dictionary of
   Contemporary Usage

Roget's II: The New Thesaurus
Shorter Oxford English
   Dictionary
Supplement to the Oxford
   English Dictionary
Webster's New Collegiate
   Dictionary
World Book Dictionary

Directories Listed in Three Textbooks (none listed by all four)

Congressional Directory
Encyclopedia of Associations

Hotel and Motel Red Book

Encyclopedias Listed in Four Textbooks

Britannica Junior
  Encyclopedia
Collier's Encyclopedia

Compton's Encyclopedia
  and Fact Index
Encyclopedia Americana

Merit Student's
  Encyclopedia
New Encyclopaedia
  Britannica
World Book Encyclopedia

Encyclopedias Listed in Three Yearbooks

Academic American
  Encyclopedia
Bol'shaia Sovetskaia
  Entsiklopediia
Brockhaus Enzyklopädie
Dictionary of American
  History
Enciclopedia Italiana

Enciclopedia Universal
  Illustrada Europeo-
  Americana
Encyclopedia of World
  Art
Great Soviet Encyclopedia

International Encyclopedia
  of the Social Sciences
McGraw-Hill Encyclopedia
  of Science and Technology
New Book of Knowledge
New Columbia
  Encyclopedia
New Grove Dictionary
  of Music and Musicians
Random House
  Encyclopedia

Geographical Sources Listed in Four Textbooks

Goode's World Atlas

Hammond Medallion World
  Atlas
National Geographic Atlas
  of the World

Rand McNally Commercial
  Atlas and Marketing
  Guide
Times Atlas of the
  World
Webster's New Geographical
  Dictionary

Goegraphical Sources Listed in Three Textbooks

American Place Names

Shepherd's Historical
  Atlas

100 *OPPORTUNITIES FOR REFERENCE SERVICES*

Columbia Lippincott
 Gazetteer

Rand McNally Cosmopolitan
 World Atlas

Times Atlas of
 World History

Guides Listed in Four Textbooks

Encyclopedia Buying
 Guide

Introdiction to United
 States Public Documents
 (Morehead)

Reader's Adviser

Guides Listed in Three Textbooks

American Reference Books
 Annual

Dictionary Buying Guide

Guide to Reference
 Books

Magazines for Libraries

New Guide to Popular
 Government Publications
 (Newsome)

Popular Guide to Government
 Publications (Leidy)

Walford's Guide to Reference
 Materials

Handbooks Listed in Four Textbooks

Bartlett's Familiar
 Quotations

Historical Statistics of the
 United States

Handbooks Listed in Three Textbooks

Famous First Facts

Guiness Book of
 World Records

Home Book of Quotations

Oxford Companion to
 English Literature

United States Government
 Manual

Indexes/Abstracts Listed in Four Textbooks

Library Literature

New York Times
 Index

Public Affairs Information
 Service

Reader's Guide to Periodical
 Literature

Indexes/Abstracts Listed in Three Textbooks

Abridged Reader's Guide	General Science Index
Access	Granger's Index to Poetry
American Statistics Index	Humanities Index
Applied Science & Technology Index	Library and Information Science Abstracts
Art Index	Magazine Index
Bibliographic Index	National Newspaper Index
Book Review Digest	Nineteenth Century Reader's Guide
Book Review Index	Play Index
Catholic Periodical Index	Poole's Index to Periodical Literature
Christian Science Monitor, Subject Index	Popular Periodical Index
Current Book Review Citations	Short Story Index
Education Index	Social Sciences Index
Essay & General Literature Index	Statistics Sources

Library/Book Trade Journals Listed in Four Textbooks

Publishers Weekly

Library/Book Trade Journals Listed in Three Textbooks

American Libraries	Reference and Subscription Books Reviews
Booklist	Reference Services Review
Choice	RQ
Library Journal	Wilson Library Bulletin

News Services Listed in Four Textbooks

Facts on File

News Services Listed in Three Textbooks

Keesing's Contemporary Archives

Yearbooks Listed in Four Textbooks

Book of the States
Britannica Book of the
  Year
Information Please Almanac
Occupational Outlook
  Handbook
Reader's Digest Almanac
  and Yearbook

Statesman's Yearbook
Statistical Abstract of the
  United States
Whitaker's Almanack
World Almanac &
  Book of Facts

Yearbooks Listed in Three Textbooks

Americana Annual
Bowker Annual

Canadian Almanac &
  Directory
Collier's Yearbook
County & City Databook

Europa Yearbook
Statistical Yearbook of
  the United Nations
World Book Yearbook

Yearbook of Agriculture

Making the Connection: The Telephone as a Creative and Potent—but Underutilized— Instrument for Reference Service

Ken Kister

SUMMARY. In recent years, reference librarians have properly accorded online and CD-ROM services much attention. But the first, simplest, and often most effective telecommunications tool available to reference librarians is the familiar telephone. Unfortunately, many reference librarians do not fully utilize the great potential of the telephone as an information-gathering tool either because they lack long-distance calling capability or are reluctant to use it. Reference librarians lacking the long-distance connection are urged to work toward making it available. Examples of how the telephone can be used to expand the reference librarian's reach are provided.

During some thirty years in the library business, I've experienced the joys and frustrations of reference work from practically every perspective, including working at busy reference desks, providing bibliographic instruction, conducting online and CD-ROM searches, building reference collections, teaching reference courses at the graduate level, and evaluating various types of reference sources in such books as *Kister's Atlas Buying Guide*, *Best Encyclopedias*, and my forthcoming *Best Dictionaries*.

You might say I'm an information addict.

Not surprisingly, I find it almost impossible to pass up any opportunity to talk with reference librarians about their work. You can

---

Ken Kister, 3118 San Juan Street, Tampa, FL 33629, is the author of various reference guides, including *Kister's Atlas Buying Guide*, *Best Encyclopedias*, and the forthcoming *Best Dictionaries* (all Oryx Press publications).

© 1991 by The Haworth Press, Inc. All rights reserved.

learn much just by listening. Recently, I ask one such librarian here in Florida if he had had any interesting questions that day, a standard icebreaker. Yes, there had been some but he was annoyed because people keep asking stupid questions.

"Stupid" questions?

"That's the kind we couldn't possibly be expected to answer. This morning, for instance, a man wanted information about what kind of fish are in Watauga Lake in Tennessee. Obviously I couldn't help him." Why not, I asked. "Well, obviously we don't carry materials here in Florida about lakes in Tennessee. I did look in several encyclopedias and found Lake Watauga on a map but nothing, naturally, about the lake's contents. I suggested the patron call a library or chamber of commerce in Tennessee — a place called Johnson City isn't far from the lake. But he didn't seem interested in doing that."

I asked the librarian why he didn't call Tennessee himself. The idea of calling a library or chamber near the lake seemed like a reasonable approach. Or, perhaps better, getting on to the appropriate state agency (e.g., fish and game commission) by consulting that wonderful little source entitled *State Administrative Officials Classified by Function* (published annually since 1967 by the Council of State Governments).

You just pick up the phone, touch the numbers, and presto, you're connected with Tennessee.

It was then that the dirty little secret came out: Our librarian confessed that he is not permitted to make long-distance calls in the name of reference.

How often I have heard this rueful story. Each time it makes me sad and angry. Put bluntly, it is a scandal that so many reference librarians must try to provide decent professional service without being able to make long-distance telephone calls when necessary or desirable.

During the past decade or so, the library profession has been abuzz with the wonders of telecommunications, computers, CD-ROM disks, online services, log-on procedures, proximity searching, boolean logic, and the like. It's all very impressive, being on the cutting edge of the electronic revolution. If nothing else, a librarian working at a terminal is held in considerably more esteem by patrons (make that clients) than one sitting at a desk shuffling 3 × 5 cards. And there can be no doubt that computerization has, and is, changing the landscape of librarianship, often for the better. I can personally testify, for example, to the efficacy of online catalogs and database searching.

But sometimes lost or forgotten among the high-tech glitz is the first, simplest, and often most useful telecommunications tool available to librarians, the familiar telephone.

AN ANCIENT TECHNOLOGY

The telephone is now about 115 years old. Recently called (hyperbolically) "the greatest invention in the history of the world" in an essay by Lance Morrow (*Time*, January 29, 1990, p. 84), phones are found in every library and on just about every library employee's desk, an essential instrument in nearly all phases of library work. Yet, perhaps due to its age or ubiquity or both, the telephone is not thought of as marvelous or glamorous but as simply a piece of furniture; librarians talk smartly about baud rates and floppy disks but not about the telephone. In fact, the phone, even today's colorful push-button variety that bleats instead of rings, tends to be perceived as old-fashioned, an appurtenance of a bygone era. As Morrow notes in his *Time* essay, "To bring electronic mysticism to the telephone may seem something like illustrating the wonders of flight by discussing pigeons."

In my experience, librarians have never sufficiently recognized or promoted the telephone as the powerful and creative information-gathering tool it can be. Too many library administrators, including some heads of reference departments, give scant if any attention to the need to equip their reference staffs with long-distance calling capability. In some instances, reference librarians have the capability but refuse to use it, believing that it is not their job to go beyond the resources of the library at and. Likewise, library school reference courses and texts tend to neglect discussion of the telephone's great potential for tracking down information across all sorts of boundaries and obstacles. The phrase "telephone reference" almost exclusively refers to that service when patrons call the library for answers to their questions, not librarians' using the phone aggressively to ferret out information.

A strong argument can be made that, in the right hands and circumstances, the telephone is currently the most effective and exciting telecommunications tool available to reference librarians. Depending on the type of question or information sought, the telephone can provide answers as quickly or more quickly than an online search. Telephone costs are usually less than those incurred for online searches. Information gathered by phone is normally more current or certainly as current as that obtained via the online route. Tina Roose, writing in *Library Journal* (December 1989, p. 89), puts it this way: "Telephone information often comes from human resources who possess the latest, most recent, not-yet-published information on a subject." Finally, the telephone is a completely interactive communications device, allowing the librarian-investigator to ask questions, clarify responses, and probe for follow-up information in a fashion no online or CD-ROM system can begin to equal.

TRUE STORIES

Here are some real-life examples that illustrate how effective—and relatively simple—the long-distance reference connection can be:

*A week after the USS Stark lost 37 crewmen in 1987 in an incident in the Persian Gulf, the local Post Office is flying the flag at full mast whereas City Hall has its flag at half-staff. The city manager wants to know which is correct?

After consulting the handy *Washington Information Directory* for the telephone number, a call to the White House in Washington DC yields the definitive answer to the question in approximately thirty seconds.

*The patron has an opportunity to bid on a used set of the first edition of the *Oxford English Dictionary* (with supplements), said to be in fair condition. What is a reasonable amount to spend for such a dictionary?

Calls to several large secondhand bookstores in New York City, including the Strand and Literary Mart, furnish a current, authoritative valuation of the now superseded 17-volume *OED*.

*The questioner is seeking the words to the national anthem of Scotland, which he believes is called "Scotland the Brave." To the librarian's surprise, the Scottish anthem is not included in the latest edition of *National Anthems of the World*, nor does this standard reference source mention "Scotland the Brave" or offer any hint why Scotland does not appear in the alphabetical sequence or the index. The country has no national anthem? A rapid check of the article on Scotland in several general encyclopedias also draws a blank on the anthem question. Next step?

A call to British Information Services in New York immediately reveals that the *official* Scottish anthem is "God Save the Queen," as Scotland is part of Great Britain. The knowledgeable BIS representative also points out that many Scots consider "Scotland the Brave" to be their true anthem and that this song may rightly be thought of as the country's *unofficial* anthem.

*A businessman needs the name and address of the president of the Carrier Corporation. *Standard & Poor's Register* provides the information but the questioner expresses concern that it might not be up-to-date, particularly in respect to the name of Carrier's president.

After considering and rejecting a database search (of the *Wall Street Journal*, Dow Jones News/Retrieval, etc.), the reference librarian calls the corporation and verifies the information in less than a minute. In the course of the transaction, the librarian obtains Carrier's nine-digit Zip Code, which is not included in *Standard & Poor's Directory*.

*An enthusiastic reader of mysteries wants to know the real name of the writer Philip DeGrave, identified as a pseudonym on the jacket of *Unholy Moses*, a Doubleday Crime Club title published in 1985. A check of several pertinent print sources, including an incomplete set of *Contemporary Authors*, proves fruitless.

A call to the editor of Doubleday's Crime Club, whose name and number are easily located in *Literary Market Place*, reveals that Philip DeGrave is a nom de plume used by William DeAndrea, a successful crime novelist who has won the Mystery Writers of

America Edgar Allan Poe Award several times. The patron is impressed by the librarian's detective work.

*A husband and wife ask for information about Nigeria, specifically the country's per capita income, monetary unit, exchange rate, and system of weights and measures. Such sources as *Statesman's Year-Book* and *Worldmark Encyclopedia of Nations* supply partial answers but as the transaction proceeds more questions develop concerning such matters as the reliability of Nigeria's postal system and the best method to send money to a person living in the country. It becomes clear eventually to the librarian that the questioners need to consult with someone who is conversant with contemporary Nigerian political and social customs. How to find an expert on Nigeria expeditiously?

A call to the Nigerian embassy in Washington DC yields an indifferent bureaucrat and practically no useful information, but the next call, to the U.S. State Department's Nigeria Desk (number obtained in the *Washington Information Directory*), turns up an intelligent, patient specialist on Nigeria who provides informed answers to all the couple's questions. Ultimately, it is revealed that they are makers of fine furniture who want to help a talented young carpenter in Nigeria establish his own business there.

*A mother has been told by her teenage son that a particular brand of hot dogs contains the blood cells of earthworms, said to be identified on the package label as "erythrobate." The questioner says she can't find the word "erythrobate" in her dictionary. How can I, she asks, convince my son that this business about earthworms in hot dogs is nonsense?

A call to the product's manufacturer quickly produces a scientific explanation of what is—and isn't—in that particular brand of wieners. The company's representative, who is familiar with and distressed by the earthworm rumor about his product, volunteers to send our relieved mother his explanation in writing.

LONG DISTANCE, PLEASE

The questions described here were answered quickly, efficiently, authoritatively, and economically only because long-distance telephone calling capability was available to the reference librarian on duty. Without the telephone, such questions would have been vastly more difficult to handle with the same degree of success. The same is that countless questions like these—daily fare at a busy reference desk—go unanswered every year because librarians lack the long-distance connection or are reluctant to use it.

The principal argument against long-distance calling to answer reference questions is cost. But Wide Area Telecommunications Service (or WATS) lines and similar systems now provide reasonably priced, unlimited long-distance telephone service to business, industry, government, and educational institutions, including practically all libraries that wish it. For instance, the Pinellas Park Public Library here in Florida, a medium-sized library serving roughly 45,000, pays under $20 a month as its share for a citywide WATS-type service. "It's too bad," observes Tina Roose, "that the way budgets are viewed in many not-for-profit libraries discourages phone use and encourages print and computer use, even if print and computer sources are slower and actually more expensive" (*Library Journal*, December 1989, p. 89).

Reference librarians who lack the long-distance connection are urged to lobby, bully, and fight their supervisors to provide this necessary tool for excellence in reference service. Nothing lights up the bright side of reference work more than the quick, efficient, authoritative, and economical answering of questions. The telephone—in concert with print, online, and CD-ROM sources—can and should play a vital part in illuminating the way to a brighter future for reference service.

The Evolution of Early Visions: An Historical Perspective on Today's Information Technology

James Rice

SUMMARY. If history helps us to understand the present and prepare for the future, we should view current information products and services in their historical perspective. The information industry, as we know it today, developed largely from the concepts of the American Documentation Institute (ADI), which was founded in 1937 and which became the American Society for Information Science (ASIS) in 1968.

This essay reviews the dreams of Watson Davis, founder of ADI, and the degree to which those dreams have been realized in the international information society. The evolution of those visions are evident in technology, information retrieval systems, information policy, and standards. The author also reviews the nature of the workstation called a "memex" described in 1945 by Vannevar Bush but which had been envisioned by Davis and his wife, Helen in 1935. These early visions of an end-user workstation closely resemble the current state of end-user information management that is possible today.

Many people believe that Information Science formally began with the founding of The American Documentation Institute (ADI) in 1937. The founder of ADI, Watson Davis, originally conceived of the organization as a service agency (rather than the professional association which it later became). The original members were not individuals but were representatives of societies, councils, and

---

James Rice is Associate Professor, School of Library and Information Science, The University of Iowa, Iowa City, IA 52242.

© 1991 by The Haworth Press, Inc. All rights reserved.

other institutions which participated in the various documentation services that ADI conducted.

The idea for ADI grew out of Davis' involvement with a non-profit corporation called Science Service which promoted the progress and understanding of science through bibliographic and publication activities. Davis became convinced that a new organization should be formed to bring together a variety of such services which would document the progress of science.

One of the services to be part of ADI was The Bibliofilm Service which microfilmed documents to order for users all over the world. It originally provided access to The Library of The U.S. Department of Agriculture, The Library of Congress, and The Army Medical Library. This extended to other libraries and stimulated microfilming in libraries generally.

Another service was Auxiliary Publications which involved many journals and institutions. This was the microfilm publication of refereed scientific and scholarly articles and reports. With the founding of ADI, the original documents would be deposited in the Library of Congress and the microfilm masters would be with Science Service.

Other proposed activities for the Institute included the application of microphotographic techniques to bibliographical problems, the development of better microfilm production and reading equipment, and research on documentation.[1]

Davis summarized the spirit of the organization in 1938:

> ... the scientific and scholarly agencies of America have in ADI an institution that is capable of doing what they wish in the broad field of documentation. Without the burden of private profit, with control solidly vested in America's organized intellectual world, ADI will be able to administer, organize, or operate activities that would be uneconomical for any one institution. Significantly, ADI brings into the same community of interest sectors of the intellectual world that otherwise do not often cooperate: in its councils and activities physicists, astronomers, biologists, economists, librarians, historians, bibliographers, archivists, and many other varieties of specialists come together to solve problems common to all.[2]

THE TRANSFORMATION OF ADI

By 1950, ADI had developed several major problems as an organization. There was a drastic decline in revenue because the demand for prints of ADI's microfilms had decreased. This was due to the copyright problem, the lack of publicity, the failure to add additions to its collection, and the availability of information elsewhere. There was also the fear of one or more rival organizations forming that would allow individual members. It became a growing concern that all members of ADI were representatives of institutional agencies, paid no dues, and had no voting power in the policy of the organization. Bibliofilm had ceased to be a function of ADI and the Auxiliary Publication Service had lost a great deal of momentum.[3]

At the annual meeting in 1952, under the leadership of Luther Evans, Librarian of Congress, ADI liberalized its membership requirements to allow both institutional and individual dues paying members. By the July meeting, 141 individuals and three institutions had applied to become members. Although this development transformed ADI into a professional organization, Watson Davis and many of the old members believed that this marked the end of ADI as it should be. He now saw the new organization as "just another library association."[4]

But in 1962, Davis reviewed the threads of interest that had dominated his thinking and his work over the years. There were four in particular that he saw as being central to the mission of The American Documentation Institute.[5] They are as follows:

1. One Big Library—Based on Watson Davis' concept that libraries should cooperate so that the users of any one had access to all the others. He called this a "net."
2. Auxiliary Publications—This was the concept of publishing scientific findings (especially those that were not likely to be published in journal or book form) on microfilm so that there was a simultaneous record which was inexpensive, up-to-date, and accessible. This should accomplish the ideal of providing accessibility to the documentation of all of the progress of science.
3. One Big Journal—This was Davis' idea of combining what

was already a lot of current awareness journals into one general publication of science which would be easy to read. If it were used in combination with indexing and abstracting services, journals and auxiliary publications, scientists would have total, easy access to the world's latest scientific knowledge.
4. The World Brain—This idea of H.G. Wells was embraced by Davis. It involved the organization and indexing of all of the knowledge of the world in order that it be easily accessible to scholars and scientists. Because Davis saw microfilm as the means for doing this, he had worked very hard to foster the development of effective microfilm selection devices.

Ideally, the world brain concept implied that indexing and abstracting of the record of science could then be distributed so that it would be accessible to any scientist anywhere. Full-text retrieval of source documents was still considered to be accomplished via library use (including the "net" concept) or via a centralized document delivery service.

Obviously, these ideas did not originate with Watson Davis. They go back to concepts of the universal availability of information fostered in organizations such as the International Institute of Bibliography founded in 1895 by Paul Otlet and Henri La Fontaine and Bradford's Science Museum Library in London.[6] There was a wide range of bibliographic activities, especially in Europe, which eventually led to the development and growth of organizations such as the International Bureau of Education which later merged into UNESCO and became part of its many biblio-graphic concerns.

Furthermore, in addition to being beyond the scope of any one organization, these goals could probably never be fully realized even within the information professions as a whole. But they were ideals which embodied a way of thinking about information, documentation, and access to the record of science.

When one combines the four concepts into a scenario for a given user, one can imagine browsing the current awareness journal (one big journal), consulting a centralized indexing and abstracting service (world brain), and having access to all source documentation of science (published literature combined with auxiliary publications) via library cooperation (one big library).

THE IMPACT OF THE NEW PROFESSIONAL ASSOCIATION

ADI's evolution from a centralized service agency to a professional organization is certainly in keeping with the complex needs of a diverse spectrum of information professions. Several of the people who were involved with ADI in the early years formed businesses and enterprises outside of the Association which were in the spirit of these ideals. For example, University Microfilms was founded by Eugene Power and The Institute for Scientific Information was initiated by Eugene Garfield. Furthermore, the theoretical framework which the goals imply has guided the development of many projects and information systems throughout the world.

During its history, ADI and all information institutions have been limited in their ability to supply completely open access to information because of the copyright law. If free enterprise is to work, the right to profit must be protected. The law has had the greatest impact on the duplication and distribution of full-text information. Davis, as well as many other leaders of the information professions, worked to achieve liberalization of the law to increase access to the documentation of science. But, in general the law has evolved, over the years, toward even greater protection of authors, creators, and publishers. While contributing to the quality of information, the copyright law has, necessarily, imposed constraints on the accomplishment of the original goals of ADI/ASIS.

But with this caveat, if we look at the performance of the information professions as a whole over 50 years, we can see a good deal of progress in realizing the dreams of documentalists such as Watson Davis. Given the proliferation of information and the complexity of the overall task of providing access to it, we can see that while much needs to be done, much has been done. Some of the most significant achievements have occurred with considerable synergy during the last few years. Let's look at Davis' four ideas in turn.

ONE BIG LIBRARY

The general notion of one big library has been available for many years through interlibrary loan. But use of the capability has been sketchy (usually less than one percent of circulation in a given library). This is because union listings of library collections and especially holdings information have not been widely available.

Since the development of the Machine Readable Catalog (MARC) project in the 60s, this has changed dramatically. Bibliographic utilities such as OCLC and RLIN formed by using the Library of Congress MARC database to implement shared catalog networks which have grown into enormous databases with holdings information. The National Union Catalog is now available in microfiche and various MARC databases are available in CD ROM format. Large research libraries are all converting their catalogs into machine readable form and nearly all libraries that did not begin with MARC are going back and reconverting to MARC format. Although there is no officially recognized national database, the large bibliographic utilities and the MARC database form such a database.[7]

Library automation vendors are converting their databases and systems into MARC and they are offering or developing MARC record interfaces with their software. Library cooperatives and consortia are building databases and various states and regions are assembling and combining their databases. So the bibliographic records, authority records and holdings information which provides access to all libraries are coming together. "There is on the horizon what may be the infrastructure for a national information network."[8]

Indexing information to journal and report literature has been increasing rapidly in the last 20 years through online search services. The economic barriers to global bibliographic access have been steadily breaking down as evidenced most recently by the dramatic influx of huge affordable databases on optical disk which can be searched on a microcomputer. But there are three areas of development which really remind us of Watson Davis' early descriptions of one big library.

One of these is the growth of gateways which have the potential of offering users access to a spectrum of services via only one actual system. These have increased through bibliographic utilities, online catalogs, and online search services. Gateway technology can eventually provide unlimited access to online information resources for any given information consumer. Services such as EasyNet link a growing number of disparate systems through one.[9]

The rapid growth of disparate information retrieval systems has led to the idea for a common command language for information retrieval. The International Standards Organization (ISO) and the National Information Standards Organization (NISO) have both proposed standardization of information retrieval command languages.[10] EasyNet IV has implemented parts of the ISO standard and OCLC has implemented the NISO standard in its EPIC online catalog.

A third area of development is the use of online searching "front-ends" — software packages that permit users to search several systems using only one retrieval language. The language is theoretically very user-friendly which vastly increases the potential user group of online retrieval systems. Gateways and front-ends are combined in services such as "The Answer Machine" which permits unlimited, fixed-cost, user-friendly access to over 1000 databases through any institution's local area network.

But the most noteworthy step toward one big library has been adoption and implementation of the Open Systems Interconnection (OSI) by so many organizations and vendors. Through initial development by the International Standards Organization and under the leadership of the Library of Congress, a set of international standards is being adopted which will permit the linking of *all* computer systems (not just information related systems). The link is currently operational and authority records as well as bibliographic records can now be exchanged between the heterogeneous computer systems.[11] Manufacturers such as IBM, DEC, NCR, Honeywell, Hewlet-Packard, and Data General are all in various stages of implementing these standards in their products.

OSI will not make all systems compatible but it will make all systems which conform to OSI standards capable of linking.[12] This means that the users of any one information system could have access, with the same searching language and hardware of their system, to other OSI compatible information systems. It also means that the enormous variety of disparate systems and databases can more readily share records, authority files, and user groups. Already, The Library of Congress, OCLC and RLIN are sharing authority files.

The dramatic expansion of databases, the ease of retrieval systems, and the connectivity now possible have all led to an explosive growth of local and state information systems. Union catalogs, open access projects, and interlibrary loan networks are all developing rapidly throughout the country.[13]

There are numerous microfilm and, more recently, electronic or optical disk documentation services. These include ADI's original Auxiliary Publication Service, University Microfilms International, Educational Resources Information Center (ERIC), National Technical Information Service (NTIS), legal publishing services such as West Publishing Co. and LEXIS, The Defense Technical Information Center (DTIC), *Energy Research Abstracts* (ERA), *American Statistics Index* (ASI), and many others.

All of these follow the spirit of publishing, organizing, indexing, storing, and disseminating scientific, technical, and scholarly information. During the last twenty years, they have all been evolving into more and more total retrieval systems (with indexing and source documents in a single system). We have fewer significant "fugitive" documents than ever before and, given the proliferation of information, this is a noteworthy level of success during 50 years.

ONE BIG JOURNAL

This concept has, in its pure sense, remained an unrealized dream. The single publication which comes closest is *The Scientist* which recently began being published by the Institute for Scientific Information. Given the vastness of science, however, it falls far short of Davis' vision.

But, in terms of becoming aware of the progress of scientific achievement in a given area, *Current Contents* should be mentioned. Clearly, it departs from Davis' "one big journal" concept because it is not a readable publication which summarizes the activities of all of science in one source. But, for any given specialty area, it does accomplish the basic objective of the concept. A scientist can browse the issues of *Current Contents* and get some pretty good ideas of what is going on within a particular field or discipline. One could argue that it accomplishes what Davis intended in a less readable and somewhat more cumbersome way for various targeted audiences.

Other important examples of publications similar to *Current Contents* are *Journal of Economic Literature*, *Psychological Abstracts*, *Biological Abstracts*, *Chemical Abstracts*, *Exerpta Medica*, *Information Abstracts*, and the abstracting journals of the publication services discussed in the previous section (such as ERIC, NTIS, and ERA).

The notion of a world brain had been "in the air" for a long time before Davis espoused it for ADI. In 1935, his wife, Helen Miles Davis, made a proposal that Science Service could develop a collection of abstracts of all the scientific articles ever printed and index them. They could then, through effective retrieval devices, "be selected easily, quickly and as automatically as possible. The original articles, moreover, must be available, in either their original form or as photographic copies. . . obviously, this cannot be created all at once."[14]

"World brain" was coined by H.G. Wells as a romanticized term for the idea of world-wide or universal bibliography — a single or coordinated bibliographic effort which could control all scientific information. In 1962, after ADI had been a professional organization for ten years, Davis had this to say:

> Organizing the knowledge of the world is still the prime need that could be filled by documentation . . . The great computer and information systems, added to advanced microfilm, developed in recent years, makes this more technically possible . . . Shall we read the plans of the past decades and then proceed to build them with the tools that were not then fashioned?[15]

The world brain concept hinges on the other three concepts. It is, in a sense, the amalgamation of all efforts toward bibliography brought to the individual scientist when and where information is needed. It represents the ability of any scientist to become aware of relevant information and have access to it as efficiently as possible. Initially, it involves only bibliographic and indexing information, but eventually, it will include full-text source information. Obviously, the copyright law must be kept in mind here.

The world brain concept also initially involves the acquisition and organization of the knowledge itself, but eventually, it includes bringing the bibliographic as well as the source information directly to the individual. The individual is what we are now calling the end-user.

It is important to note the development of CD ROM databases and their impact on the world brain idea. At some point, assuming limitations imposed by the copyright law, we can expect that scientists will have specialized desktop CD ROM databases of full-text information relevant to their disciplines. Even now, hundreds of reference tools including encyclopedias, directories, online catalogs, indexing and abstracting services, and some full-text databases are available in CD ROM form.

Both Watson Davis and later Vannevar Bush saw the organization of the world's knowledge as being closely linked with the concept of access to that knowledge by the individual user. Davis' notion was that a device would be located at a central site (such as ADI) and would store a large collection of information in microfilm. The information would be retrieved by specialists on order and sent to the user. Davis described such a device in 1935 although there is evidence that the original idea for it was developed jointly by Davis, his wife, Helen Davis and a colleague who specialized in equipment design, R.H. Draeger. The device was to be used in the Bibliofilm service.[16]

Vannevar Bush later described a similar device, the "memex," in his famous article "As We May Think."[17] Bush had initiated the development of a "Rapid Selector" in 1936 which was later patented in 1942.[18] Bush's concept, however, was significantly different from that of Davis, especially from the standpoint of end-user information retrieval.

THE MEMEX

The memex was . . .

> a device in which an individual stores all his books, records, and communications, and which is mechanized so that it may be consulted with exceeding speed and flexibility. It is an enlarged intimate supplement to his memory. It consists of a desk, and while it can presumably be operated from a distance, it is primarily the piece of furniture at which he works. On the top are slanting translucent screens, on which material can be projected for convenient reading. There is a keyboard, and sets of buttons and levers. Otherwise it looks like an ordinary desk.[19]

It is clear that Bush's vision of the memex is a full-text information retrieval system which is used by the scientist unassisted. The description also implies instantaneous access and automatic connectivity between files and indexes to files. These two capabilities, full-text storage and integration of various databases, have both been missing from the full realization of the world brain idea. Interestingly, OSI, full-text information systems, and CD ROM technology are providing breakthroughs in both of these areas with an unprecedented synergy.

As microfilm based devices, the Rapid Selector, and even the visionary memex have been vastly outpaced by digital technology as manifested in microcomputers for distributed computing and information access. We have had microcomputer-based access to online searching for years. We have had downloading and uploading, the ability to store, organize, sort, print, and so forth via database management systems which import records from communication software packages. Systems such Pro-Cite (used in combination with Biblio-link), and Search Helper accomplish these functions.[20]

What is being accomplished right now, however, is the highly efficient integration of all of these functions into single, easy-to-use software packages that can access online library catalogs and online search services using the same searching languages. Records from these systems can then be instantly stored and kept by end-users who don't need much training to accomplish these capabilities.

For example, such a package has been fully developed at The University Libraries at Penn State in connection with their catalog, "The Library Information Access System" (LIAS). While it has not yet been released for campus-wide use, the system uses a simple retrieval language, autodial into the public access catalog, and high speed searching. Then, the user can download all relevant records, perform a variety of database management functions on those records, print them out in any order in footnotes, biblio-graphies, or full-record form, search these files at any time, import them into a word processor, and accomplish a host of other capabilities.[21] It is hoped that the MicroLIAS system can be released soon because it is a pioneer in this area. There are several online catalogs, however, that have similar end-user software packages which are operational.[22] Of course, the great advantage of these is that the bibliographic references match a local, readily available collection. They can also be linked to an interlibrary loan service or full-text retrieval service for journal and report literature.

From a hardware standpoint, the devices envisioned by Davis and Bush closely resemble the current desktop workstation that is being adopted by a rapidly growing number of scientists, professionals, and scholars.[23] Using the capabilities described above, these people are accomplishing end-user access to information and management of databases to incorporate into their practice, scientific studies, or scholarly output.

CONCLUSION

The developments outlined above are all coming together. Using language such as "scholar workstation" and "end-user access to information" the literature is filled with current discussions of old dreams. Information consumers can now have a workstation that is even more powerful than the futuristic "memex" described in 1945 by Vannevar Bush but which had been envisioned in part by Watson and Helen Davis in 1935. Such a workstation for end-user information management is a major benchmark in the evolution of science and scholarship.

We now have integrated, efficient, easy-to-use personal information management systems which can access an impressive and growing portion of the world's information. These tools are just now becoming available, and only a minority of the potential users actually use them. But, it appears that, over the next few years, the pipe dreams of people like Watson Davis and Vannevar Bush will become standard equipment.

REFERENCES

1. Schultz, Claire K. and Paul L. Garwig. "History of the American Documentation Institute—A Sketch" *American Documentation* Vol. 20 No. 2 (April 1969) pp. 152-153.

2. Davis, Watson. "Report of the President of American Documentation Institute, January 27, 1938" *Journal of Documentary Reproduction* Vol. 1 no.1 (Winter 1938) p. 35.

3. *Op. Cit.* Schultz and Garwig. pp. 157-158. Also see, "Report of the ADI Auxiliary Publications Program" *American Documentation* Vol. 13 No. 1 (January 1962) pp. 134-136.

4. Farcas-Conn, Irene. *From Documentation to Information Science: The Origins and Early Development of the American Documentation Institute—American Society for Information Science*, Ph.D., University of Chicago. 1984. pp. 469-470.

5. *Op. Cit.* Schultz and Garwig. p. 154.

6. *Op. Cit.* Farcas-Conn, Irene. p. 472.

7. Molholt, Pat. *Library Networking: The Interface of Ideas and Actions.* Working Paper—Rensselaer Polytechnic Institute funded by the U.S. Department of Education. (June 1988) p. 12.

8. Sugnet, Chris. "Networking in Transition: Current and Future Issues" *Library Hi Tech* Vol. 6 (Issue 24) 1988. p.101.

9. Burton, Hilary D. "Virtual Information Systems: Unlimited Resources for Information Retrieval" *The Reference Librarian* No. 22, 1988. pp. 127-128.

10. Tenopir, Carol. "A Common Command Language" *Library Journal* Vol. 114. No. 8 (May 1, 1989) p. 56.

11. For a brief overview of the development of OSI, see Avram, Henriette D. "Toward a Nationwide Library Network" *Journal of Library Administration* Vol. 8 Numbers 3/4 (Fall-Winter 1987) pp. 93-114. For discussions of actual implementation, see Buckland, Michael K. and Clifford A. Lynch. "The Linked Systems Protocol and the Future of Bibliographic Networks and Systems" *Information Technology and Libraries* Vol. 6 No. 2 (June 1987) pp. 83-88. and

Boss, Richard W. "Linked Systems and the Online Catalog: The Role of the OSI" *Library Resources and Technical Services* Vol. 34 No. 2. (April 1990) pp. 217-228.

12. Denenberg, Ray. "Open Systems Interconnection" *Library Hi Tech* vol. 3 (Issue 9) 1985. pp. 16-24. Also see subsequent articles on the Linked Systems Project and the OSI in Issues 10 and 13 of *Library Hi Tech*.

13. Kallenbach, Susan. "Local Systems Implementation of the OSI Reference Model: The NYU/RLG Project" *Bookmark* Vol. 76 No. 11. (Winter 1988) p. 109. Also see, Hildreth, Charles R. "Library Networking in North America in the 1980s. Part 1: The dreams; the realities" *The Electronic Library* Vol. 5 No. 4. (August 1987) p. 226.

14. *Op. Cit*. Schultz and Garwig. p. 154.

15. *Ibid*.

16. *Op. Cit*. Farcas-Conn, Irene. pp. 116.

17. Bush, Vannevar. "As We May Think" *The Atlantic Monthly* Vol. 176. No. 1 (July 1945) pp. 101-108.

18. Wiesner, Jerome B. "Vannevar Bush" *Biographical Memoirs* National Academy of Sciences Vol. 50 1979. p. 103.

19. *Op. Cit*. Bush, pp. 106-107.

20. Rice, James. "End-user Management of Information from Online Search Services and Online Public Access Catalogs" *Microcomputers for Information Management* Vol. 4 No. 4 (December, 1987). pp. 309-310.

21. Carson, Sylvia Mackinnon, & Freivalds, Dace I. "MicroLIAS: Beyond the online public access catalog" *Library Hi Tech* Vol. 4 (Issue 15) 1986 pp. 83-90.

22. Rice, James. "Microcomputer Database Management Systems which Interface to Online Public Access Catalogs" *Reference Services Review* Vol. 16. Numbers 1-2, 1988 pp. 57-60.

23. Weiskel, Timothy C. "University Libraries, Integrated Scholarly Information Systems (ISIS), and the Changing Character of Academic Research" *Library Hi Tech* Vol. 6 No. 4. (Issue 24) 1988. p. 7.

The Library of Congress Remote Online Library User Pilot Project: The California State Library Experience

Kathleen Low

SUMMARY. In August of 1989, the Library of Congress selected fourteen libraries nationwide to participate in a pilot project to test and determine the feasibility and desirability of remote online access to the Library's information system. The California State Library was selected as one of the participant libraries. During the project, State Library staff performed 187 subject searches on various topics in the Library of Congress Information System (LOCIS). LOCIS was easy to search, and contained a variety of useful search features. Overall, staff found access to LOCIS to be a valuable addition to our existing online search services.

In 1988 Librarian of Congress James Billington held eleven Management and Planning Forums across the nation. In each of the meetings he received numerous requests from librarians desiring access to the Library of Congress' online computer system. In response to these requests, Dr. Billington sought, and received, congressional authorization for a six month pilot project to help the Library test and determine the feasibility and desirability of remote online access to the Library's information system. A team of thirteen reference and automation experts from the Library of Congress was brought together to plan what became known as the ROLLUP (Remote Online Library User Pilot) Project.

In July the ROLLUP project was announced and applications

Kathleen Low is Outreach Services Manager at the California State Library, State Information & Reference Center, P.O. Box 942837, Sacramento, CA 94237-0001.

were sought from academic, public and research libraries interested in becoming test sites. Selection of the test sites would be based upon the following criteria:

1. long-term experience with and commitment to online database access
2. experience in providing online access and training to library patrons
3. staff resources to train library patrons to use the Library of Congress System
4. institutional resources to pay for telecommunications costs
5. hardware and software necessary to connect to the Library of Congress system
6. financial commitment to send one staff member to the Library for a two-day training session
7. willingness to compile test and cost data.

In addition, applicants were to provide a short statement describing what potential benefits they expected to receive from access to the system, and a physical description of the environment in which the library's reference services take place, to the Library of Congress. The deadline for applications was August 21, 1989.

Eight test sites were to be selected. However, because of the volume of applications received, fourteen libraries were selected from the sixty-three applications received. The libraries selected were: Boston Public Library, California State Library, District of Columbia Public Library, Duke University, Florida State University School of Library and Information Studies, Lehigh University, Los Alamos National Laboratory, New York State Library, Oregon State Library, University of Kentucky/Kentucky State Library, University of Maryland, University of Michigan, University of Southern California, U.S. Information Agency (see Appendix A).

On September 21-22, 1989, a representative from each of the participating libraries converged upon the Library of Congress for intensive hands-on training in the Library of Congress Information System (LOCIS). The purpose of the training was not only to instruct participants in searching LOCIS, but to provide them with the knowledge and materials necessary for them to train staff in their respective libraries. The training was presented by ROLLUP Team members Louis Drummond of the Congressional Research Service, Ron Bluestone of the General Reading Rooms Division, Dave Eastridge of the Copyright Office, and Maryle Ashley of the Information Technology Services Directorate. Throughout the training participants were supplied with copies of handouts and user manuals as needed to train their respective staffs.

The first day of the training focused on the telecommunication options for accessing LOCIS, the logon procedures, an overview of LOCIS, an introduction to the MUMS subsystem, and the procedures for searching the MUMS subsystem. The second day focused on the files in the SCORPIO subsystem, its search protocols, and data to be submitted to the Library of Congress. On both days, participants received hands-on practice and exercises.

The project officially began October 1, 1989 with an ending date of March 30, 1990. During the project though, many of the participating libraries expressed concern that their access to LOCIS would end two months short of the academic year. Although only seven of the participants are academic libraries, all but one of the fourteen libraries provide direct service to students as part of their clientele. The project was therefore extended until May 30, 1990, according to Dr. Billington, "to see our partners through the academic year, as well as to gain additional information to evaluate the project."[1]

Two systems comprise the Library of Congress Information System—the Multiple Use MARC System (MUMS) and the Subject Content Oriented Retriever for Processing Information Online (SCORPIO). MUMS was originally intended for cataloging purposes whereas SCORPIO was designed for public reference use. Each system utilizes its own separate search protocols.

SCORPIO

SCORPIO embodies six files: the Legislative Information Files (CG), the Bibliographic Citation File (BIBL), the National Referral Master File (NRCM), the Copyright Files (COHM, COHD, COHS), the Books File (LCCC), and the PREMARC File (PREM).

Legislative Information Files

The Legislative Information Files contain information on the status of federal legislation from the 93rd Congress (1973) to present. Each file contains and traces the status of each bill and includes a digest. The following information can be found in the file: the bill's sponsor, cosponsor, or amendment sponsor, an abstract of the bill, committee information (including originating, and the committee to which it was referred), a chronology of major bill actions after reported to committee, amendments, and the text of public laws as appropriate. These files are the electronic equivalent of the *Digest of Public General Bills and Resolutions*, and are updated on a daily basis. (Note that the full text of the bills is not online.)

Information in these files can be retrieved by Congress member's name, bill or public law number, committee of referral, or by subject term. (Subject terms used are those listed in the printed *Legislative Indexing Vocabulary Terms (LIVT) Thesaurus*.)

Bibliographic Citation File (BIBL)

The Bibliographic Citation File selectively lists periodical articles, U.S. government documents, and United Nations publications in the areas of public policy and current affairs since 1976. Over 750 journals, such as *The Journal of Finance*, *JAMA*, and *The Middle East Journal*, are scanned for pertinent articles. Each citation contains standard bibliographic data plus an abstract written by Congressional Research Service staff. The records for U.S. government publications, however, do not list the GPO catalog number.

BIBL can be searched by author, title, publication, publication year, words within the title or abstract, or subject terms from the *LIVT Thesaurus*. Information in BIBL is updated on a weekly basis.

National Referral Center Master File (NRCM)

The National Referral Center Master File provides information on over 14,000 qualified organizations willing to provide information to the general public. The file is based upon a national inventory program that began in 1962. The organizations included in the file are either performing research in their respective fields, or maintain special resources in the area. The primary focus of the file is on science, technology, and the social sciences.

Each listing contains the basic contact information such as the organization's name, address and telephone number. Also included is the organization's area(s) of interest, collection holdings, and any publications issued by them. Information on services provided and any limitations to those services is provided as well. The file is updated twice a month.

The file can be searched by organization name, or by subject terms. A separate subject thesaurus is issued for this file.

Copyright Files

A variety of copyright information can be found in the Copyright History Documents File (COHD), the Copyright History Monographs File (COHM), and the Copyright History Serials File (COHS). Literary works, works of performing and visual arts, and sound recordings registered in the Copyright Office since January 1, 1978 can be found in the Copyright History Monographs file. Renewals of previously copyrighted works are included, however serial records are not. A typical record includes the copyright claimant, the author, title, registration date and class, and the imprint date.

There are four approaches to access the COHM file. It can be searched by the claimant's name, the author's name, by title, or by copyright registration number.

Copyright registrations for serials and periodicals are located in the Copyright History Serials File (COHS). Records in this file contain the title, edition statement, imprint, frequency of publication, ISSN, and key title. For each issue of a serial, data is provided on the claimant's name, registration number, date of registration, volume and issue number, issue date, date of creation, and date of publication.

Complementing the COHM and COHS files is the Copyright History Documents File (COHD). The Documents File functions as an index to the legal records on file in the Copyright Office. COHD facilitates finding information on the author's pseudonyms, whether the author is alive or dead, copyright termination notices, and transfers of copyright. Each record also includes the names of the parties involved, date of recordation and execution, and the title of the work involved.

All three copyright files are updated on a weekly basis.

Library of Congress Computerized Catalog (LCCC)

The Library of Congress Computerized Catalog (LCCC) in SCORPIO is known as the BOOKS file in the Multiple-Use-MARC System (MUMS). LCCC can be searched in either system. The file contains records for books cataloged or recataloged by the Library of Congress for books in English since 1968, in French from 1973, in German, Portuguese and Spanish since 1975, with other European languages since 1976, with some non-English languages since 1978, in all languages since 1980, and some microfilms since 1984. In some cases, the Library of Congress will create catalog records for books it has opted to not add to its collection.

Except for books assigned minimal level cataloging, each record contains full catalog information. These records can be retrieved by author, title, subject, partial Library of Congress call number, and Library of Congress card number. Search results can be limited by a wide range of factors including the language of the publication, year of publication, type of publication (i.e., government publication, etc.), by type of illustration included, etc.

PREMARC File

Records for older Library of Congress materials cataloged before those dates listed in the LCCC file can be found in the PREMARC File. The PREMARC File embodies Library of Congress records since 1898 for not only books, but serials, maps, and music scores as well. Searchers of this file should be advised that the file is incomplete and contains various errors. Access points for this file are the same as for the LCCC file.

MULTIPLE USE MARC SYSTEM (MUMS)

The Multiple Use MARC System was originally designed for internal cataloging purposes. It uses highly structured commands to retrieve data. Because the records in this system represent such a wide range and wealth of resources available at the Library of Congress, it is an invaluable reference tool as well as a cataloging tool. It should again be noted that there may be some records in the system for items the Library has opted not to retain in its collection.

The system contains the following files:

Serials File

This file contains records for serials cataloged by the Library of Congress or other libraries since 1973.

Serials Locations (SERLOC)

Records in the SERLOC file indicate if the Library of Congress is retaining a serial, but does not include information on individual issues received.

Maps File

This file contains records for printed and manuscript cartographic materials held by the Library and cataloged since 1968, and reports of maps by some other libraries since 1985. These records reflect sheet maps, relief models, and globes.

Music File

Records for music and sound recordings (musical and spoken word) cataloged at the Library since 1984 are found in the MUSIC File. Records in this file contain notes identifying performers when applicable.

Audiovisual File

Within this file, searchers can find records for filmstrips, motion pictures, videorecordings, slide sets, transparencies, photographs, prints, and drawings cataloged selectively since 1972.

National Union Catalog

The National Union Catalog File includes records for books cataloged at selected libraries and reported to the Library of Congress since late 1982. Some of these records represent items which may be in the Library of Congress, but were cataloged prior to the Library obtaining a copy of the item.

National Register of Additional Locations

This file contains book holdings information from other libraries that has been reported to the Library of Congress since 1968 (with imprint dates later than 1954).

Near East National Union List

The file contains records for selected books and serials before 1979 in Arabic, Persian, Ottoman Turkish, and modern Turkish held by approximately 240 institutions in the U.S. and Canada. About half the items listed in the file are available at the Library of Congress.

Books Master File

This BOOKS MASTER FILE is the same file as the LCCC file in the SCORPIO system. Records in this file are displayed in the MARC format.

Automated Process Information File

This file contains preliminary catalog records for both books that have been received in the Library of Congress, and those not yet received or published.

Library Order Information System

Brief records for items that are being purchased by the Library can be found in this file.

Manuscripts

This file contains over 13,000 "collection level" records for most of the collections in the Library of Congress' Manuscripts Division.

Computer Files

Machine readable catalog records for materials in machine readable form (software, etc.) can be located in this file.

Generalized Bibliography Application File

Originally designed for production of internal bibliographies, the file contains selected records of materials in the various reading rooms.

SEARCH STRUCTURES

SCORPIO files can be searched using a simple set of commands. The basic command structure is the word "browse" followed by a word or words. The browse command searches for the term as it appears as the first word in the author, title, or subject index. Records retrieved as a result of the browse command are stored in a set. Searchers can then display the citations within a set in either a brief or full format. The search sets can be combined with other search sets using boolean operators. Sets may also be further refined by limiting the records within a set by a variety of options, such as language, date, and types of illustrations included, depending upon the file searched.

Data can be retrieved from MUMS by either keyword searching, or compression searching. New or occasional users can search for keywords which appear in the author, title, subject, series, or note files of catalog records, while more sophisticated users can benefit from compression searching. In compression searching, a designated number of letters are combined from the title, author's name, etc. to form a search string which can be restricted to a specific file or files, and MARC fields.

The California State Library

The California State Library was one of fourteen libraries selected to participate in the ROLLUP Project. Located in the Library and Courts Building in Sacramento, the State Library is divided into two bureaus: the Library Development Services Bureau, and the

State Library Services Bureau. The Library Development Services Bureau provides technical assistance to libraries and also administers federal and state grant programs, while the State Library Services Bureau provides direct library service to state agencies and the legislature, serves as a backup resource to libraries throughout the state, and assists individual researchers. The State Library Services Bureau is comprised of six public service units: the Sutro Library (located in San Francisco), the Braille and Talking Book Library (located blocks away from the Library and Courts Building), the Government Publications Section, the California Section, the State Information and Reference Center, and the Law Library.

The Law Library maintains California and United States codes and statutes, court reports, administrative regulations, law reviews and other standard legal materials. The Law Library also collects California legislative bills, state Appellate and Supreme Court briefs, and primary source materials from all fifty states. California city and county charters, codes, and ordinances can also be located in the Law Library.

Documents, from the local to federal level, can be found in the Government Publications Section. The Library is a complete depository for state publications, and the only full depository of Government Printing Office publications in California. The Government Publications Section houses over 200,000 local and state publications, and over 2.3 million federal documents.

One of the State Library's missions is also "to collect, preserve and disseminate information regarding the history of the state."[2] The California Section fulfills this mission by actively collecting materials (both book and nonbook) on all aspects of life in the state from prehistoric times to the present day. The section maintains a particularly strong collection on the gold rush period, the Mother Lode, mines and mining, business and government, and California genealogy.

The State Information and Reference Center maintains the library's core research collection. It provides resources in a variety of disciplines with special emphasis on topics of interest to state government. In addition, the Center also operates a branch library in the State Capitol.

Located several blocks away from the Library and Courts Building is the Braille and Talking Book Library. The Braille and Talking Book Library, in cooperation with the Library of Congress National Library Service for the Blind and Physically Handicapped, lends recorded and braille books to Northern Californians unable to read standard print. The library also maintains information on blindness, visual impairments and other physical disabilities.

The Sutro Library, a branch of the State Library located in San Francisco, provides patrons access to materials in genealogy and local history, including family histories, local histories, and indexes to pre-1900 ship passenger arrival lists for major eastern ports. The library grew from the rare book collection of Adolph Sutro which was donated to the state by his heirs. The collection is particularly strong in Mexican and English history, the history of science and technology, and voyages and travel.

ONLINE SEARCH SERVICES

As part of our public services, the library has offered mediated online database search services to state employees since 1973. At present, the library has access to the following commercial online systems: BRS, DIALOG Information Services, Mead Data Central's LEXIS/NEXIS, VuText, DataTimes, NewsNet, National Library of Medicine's MEDLARS System, Pergamon ORBIT, LEGI-TECH, as well as the National Conference of State Legislature's Integrated States Information System (ISIS). The library also has access to CASSIS, RLIN, and the University of California Library System's MELVYL Online Catalog.

Library staff perform online database searches for: (1) state employees working on state business when it is the best method of obtaining the information needed, and (2) to answer ready reference questions received at the reference desk when it is the best method of obtaining the answer. Staff formulate the search strategy, select the appropriate databases, perform the search, and provide the patron with a printout of the results. There is no charge to the patron for this service.

At the start of the project, fourteen public service librarians and four technical service librarians were trained to search LOCIS. The librarians in the State Information and Reference Center perform the bulk of the online searches received at the library. These librarians were instructed to search LOCIS as needed in response to reference requests received regardless of whether or not the patron was a state government employee or not. The library's ability to access LOCIS was announced to both state government and to libraries in the state. An article on the library's ability to access LOCIS appeared in the *California State Library Newsletter* which is distributed to public, academic, and special libraries throughout the state. Further information on our participation in the project was provided to reference coordinators from the various library public systems at one of their semi-annual meetings. A letter and flyer were also mailed to every state legislator notifying them of our participation in the pilot project, and our ability to search LOCIS as needed, or upon request.

During the eight month pilot project, library staff performed 187 subject searches on topics ranging from campaign finance reform to septic tank alternatives. The bulk of the searches was performed in the Bibliographic Citation File and Library of Congress Computerized Catalog File. The majority of those searches were performed for either legislative or state agency staff.

Library staff have also received various requests from attorneys and writers throughout the state for information on the copyright holders of assorted films, radio shows, and television series. Since each episode of a television series is usually copyrighted, these files can also be used to generate a list of the episodes in a series. The information in the copyright files seems to be of most interest to the general public since it is not as readily accessible as some of the other data. And the currency of this file makes it especially valuable.

Reference staff found the Bibliographic Citation File (BIBL) and the Library of Congress Computerized Catalog (LCCC) files particularly useful in their work. The BIBL file is often searched for citations to relevant information gathered in response to subject requests. The coverage of the file is pertinent to many of our requests since topics of interest to federal legislators are also of interest to state legislators. And the ability to search one source containing citations to both journal articles and federal publications is very convenient, since most commercial databases do not include extensive government publications. For these reasons, staff have also used it to gather background information for various topical annotated bibliographies produced by the Reference Center.

The LCCC file is also used on a fairly regular basis, because of the ability to limit search sets not only by the language of the publication, but by the year and place of publication, by the type of publication (biographical, conference proceeding, government publication), by contents notes, by illustration, and by intellectual level as well. The file is very useful for bibliographic verification, or for locating subject materials in a specific language.

Cataloging staff in the library were also trained to search the MUMS files. However, they found no major advantage to searching LOCIS over RLIN, our online cataloging utility, due to the rapid speed with which LC MARC data appears in RLIN.

After searching the system for a few months, reference staff identified three enhancements they would like to see added to LOCIS. The first pertains to the copyright files. It would be useful if the copyright files contained an online help screen which described the various abbreviations used for each field (such as CLNA = claimant's name, etc.). Second, it would be nice if a display option could be added in which records in the BIBL file would display the full citation and subject thesaurus terms only (not the notes or the "bucket" terms). And last, GPO document numbers should be added to appropriate records in the BIBL file.

Overall, we have found LOCIS to be a good source for a variety of information. It's easy to use, and contains a variety of useful search features. It also provides us with a method of retrieving current data not yet available in printed form. Our ability to access LOCIS during the project was a valuable addition to our existing online search services.

CONCLUSION

Suzanne Thorin, Library of Congress Pilot Project Coordinator, in highlighting the final report of the pilot group, said, "We found that we need a longer experiment with a larger group of users, to enable us to evaluate more fully the impact on the Congress of providing online access to remote users. We also found that, because state library agencies are mandated to meet the information needs of state legislatures and to facilitate the development of statewide library services, our strongest user group in the pilot was comprised of the four state libraries: California, New York, Oregon, and Kentucky."

"Because we believe that the state library agencies are the logical organizations through which to test further the need to provide online access at remote sites, the Librarian of Congress, James H. Billington, has requested the approval of the Joint Committee on the Library to begin a two-year pilot with the 50 state library agencies and the District of Columbia Public Library (acting as the District's library development agency)."

REFERENCES

1. "Library of Congress Extends Remote Access Pilot Project," Library of Congress, Washington, DC 3/26/90. Press Release.
2. California. Education Code 19320(h)

APPENDIX A

ROLLUP PARTICIPANT LIBRARIES

Boston Public Library
Copley Square
Boston, MA 02217

California State Library
914 Capitol Mall
Sacramento, CA 95814

District of Columbia Public Library
901 G St. N.W.
Washington, DC 20001

Duke University
Perkins Library
Durham, NC 27706

Florida State University
School of Library and Information Studies
Tallahassee, FL 32306

Lehigh University
464 Fairchild-Martindale Library
Bethlehem, PA 18015

Los Alamos National Laboratory Library
P.O. Box 1663, P-362
Los Alamos, NM 87545

New York State Library
Empire State Plaza
Reference-6th Floor
Albany, NY 12231

Oregon State Library
State Library Building
Salem, OR 97310

U.S. Information Agency
Agency Library
301 4th St. SW, Room 135
Washington, DC 20547

University of Kentucky Libraries
Lexington, KY 40506-0039

University of Maryland
McKeldin Reference
College Park, MD 20742

University of Michigan
Hatcher Graduate Library
Ann Arbor, MI 48109

University of Southern California
University Park
Los Angeles, CA 90089-0182

APPENDIX B

LIBRARY OF CONGRESS ROLLUP TEAM MEMBERS

Suzanne Thorin	General Reading Rooms Division (202) 707-5530
Maryle Ashley	Information Technology Services Directorate (202) 707-9641
Ron Bluestone	General Reading Rooms Division/MMR (202) 707-5525

Sharon Butts	Congressional Research Service (202) 225-2424
Erik Delfino	Federal Library and Information Center Committee (202) 707-1374
Louis Drummond	Congressional Research Service (202) 707-2482
David Eastridge	Copyright Office (202) 707-5294
Judith Farley	General Reading Rooms Division/MMR (202) 707-8475
Sally McCallum	Network Development Office (202) 707-6237
Teresa Meikle	Science and Technology Division (202) 707-1193
Gail Sonnemann	Cataloging Distribution Service (202) 707-1287
David Tilghman	Loan Division (202) 707-7994
Hazel Williams	Serial Record Division (202) 707-6686

APPENDIX C

Sample Full Display of a BIBL file record.

LOCATION:	LRS90-3049
AUTHOR:	U.S. General Accounting Office.
TITLE:	Puerto Rico: commonwealth election law and its application to a political status referendum. May 1990.
SOURCE:	Washington, G.A.O., 1990. 64 p.
NOTES:	"GAO/HRD-90-60, B-235508

Answers the following questions: "How are Puerto Rico's elections administered? What safeguards and controls exist to assure the integrity of election results? What roles do the U.S. Department of Justice and Federal Election Commission have in Puerto Rico's elections? What limitations are placed on campaign financing in Puerto Rico and how are they administered? What are the rights of nonresident Puerto Ricans to participate in the status referendum? What problems have been experienced in past elections?"

SUBJECT(S):	Referendum—Puerto Rico
	Election administration—Puerto Rico
	Campaign funds—Puerto Rico
	Statehood (American politics)—Puerto Rico
	Sovereignty—Puerto Rico
	National self-determination—Puerto Rico
BUCKET(S):	Latin America
	Politics and elections
	Territories

APPENDIX D

Sample COHM file record

TX-453-550   (COHM)   ITEM 1 OF 1 IN SET 8

TITL:	The Stand / Stephen King.
IMPR:	New York : New American Library, ©1980.
PHYS:	817 p.
CLNA:	Stephen King
DCRE:	1979 DPUB: 9Jan80 DREG: 4Feb80
PREV:	Prev. reg. 1978, TX 141-312.
LINM:	NM: "minor revisions throughout the text."
MISC:	C.O. corres.
ECIF:	1/B/D

HPER for Help: Selection and Reference Tools for a New Field

Elaine Cox Clever
David P. Dillard

SUMMARY. A discussion of the interdisciplinary field, known in many academic circles as Health, Physical Education, and Recreation (HPER). Awareness of the central issues and problems of the field is important and the various approaches are considered. Selection of materials is a major task, and this is the central focus of the paper.

"I want to find out more about the Exxon spill and the effects of oil spills on animal life and the food chain." "I want information about pesticide contamination." " . . . the impact of nutrition and diet on health." " . . . ocean pollution at shore resorts." Examples of similar questions of current concern being asked by patrons at public and academic libraries include athletes and addiction to substances or to gambling; AIDS and the need for prevention; handling the psychological and physical rehabilitation process following serious accident or injury. In addition to current critical issues, there are always a substantial number of questions involving recreational activities, professional sports, information about travel, tourism, hobbies, participation in sports, and other leisure pursuits.

An interdisciplinary field, relatively unknown outside of the aca-

---

Elaine Cox Clever is Research Librarian at Temple University. David P. Dillard is at Temple University as Reference Librarian and Business and Sports Recreation Health Database Analyst. Ms. Clever, also, is a partner in Answers/INformation Brokers of Haddonfield, NJ. Communication with the authors should be directed to P.O. Box 2194, Haddonfield, NJ 08033.

© 1991 by The Haworth Press, Inc. All rights reserved.

demic sphere, has emerged in the last twenty years that covers much of the information pertinent to the above topics. That combined field is known in a number of colleges and universities as Health, Physical Education, and Recreation (HPER). The first two components, Health and Physical Education, had largely been step children in schools of Education. Other health programs had been confined to Public Health Schools or to Health Administration programs. Recreation was modestly covered in fields such as sociology, psychology, or history.

Why have HPER programs become so prominent in recent years at a number of academic institutions? It seems evident that academicians, as well as the public, are more keenly aware of the key changes in our lives than was true a generation ago. These changes include close attention to matters such as wellness, physical exercise, participation in sports by adults and children, nutrition, safety of our environment, and improving the quality of our leisure time. This mix of new interests closely parallels the interdisciplinary components of HPER programs. These programs vary from institution but typically provide many of the following academic offerings. Health includes topics such as public health, nutrition, substance abuse, epidemiology, consumer health, the aging process, indoor and outdoor environmental pollution, human sexuality, and mental health. Physical Education covers sports medicine, motor skills, athletic training, biomechanics, exercise physiology, coaching, history of amateur and professional sports, sports management, physical fitness business enterprise, and kinesiology. The subfields of Recreation deal with therapeutic, military, corporate, campus, commercial and private recreation, as well as leisure counseling, retirement counseling, camping and wilderness adventure programs, cultural leisure pursuits, tourism, and travel.

If one takes a moment to think about the range of interests and activities represented by this long, but not exhaustive, list of fields, one can see that we are considering areas of human concern that impinge on virtually all of our waking hours outside of the workplace and have many facets that include the workplace. Information that is so vital to our lives demands substantial support in a library collection.

A major body of literature and research has been developing simultaneously with the growth of HPER fields. This literature offers librarians a unique access point to authoritative publications, that may not have been routinely considered when seeking information on questions relevant to the multitude of topics enumerated above.

Periodicals are a prime source in a field that is both new and inter-disciplinary. A number of periodicals in this field cover multiple disciplines. While they frequently cover a broader range of subjects than those defined by HPER, indexes that include these journals make easy "one-stop shopping" for a wide range of topics. Examples of multi-disciplinary journals include the *Journal of Physical Education, Recreation and Dance* which some consider the core journal of the field; *Journal of Sports History* which can be viewed as a history journal as well as a sports journal; *Journal of Sport and Social Issues*; *Research Quarterly for Exercise and Sport*; and *Special Recreation Digest* which is aimed as much at the differently abled as it is at recreation. Other more focused titles include *Human Movement Science*, *Journal of Leisure Research*, and *Parks & Recreation*. Most of these journals tend to be non-technical and readily understandable by a general audience. However, some of the titles, particularly in biomedical, biokenetic, sports medicine, and exercise physiology fields, are quite technical and aimed at the practitioner.

When it comes to the selection of monographic materials, it has to be emphasized again that HPER is a new and developing field and that many times, for lack of other sources, textbooks cannot be overlooked. Other monographic sources include rule books for sports, handbooks that serve as overviews of specific subfields, and hands-on, how-to-do-it advice for everything from wilderness adventures, camping, sports, games, and first aid, to counseling and hobbies.

RESEARCH PROJECT MATERIALS

HPER is an academic field and much of the information comes from ongoing research projects. Excellent resource material can also be gained from organizations and associations which publish report monographs, proceedings of conferences, and research report series. Besides publications, many of these organizations can be queried directly via hotlines or 800 numbers. The *Encyclopedia of Associations* (Gale), *Research Centers Directory* (Gale), and *National Avocational Organizations* (Columbia Books) provide comprehensive directory coverage to HPER organizations.

Doctoral dissertations and masters theses have been produced at schools with HPER programs. They have been selectively published by the University of Oregon in an ongoing microfiche set. A substantial number of HPER publications are reproduced by the federal government as ERIC documents. Also under federal auspices, a surprising number of publications relevant to HPER are produced by the Government Printing Office and by the National Technical Information Service (NTIS). And, especially in the field of recreation, the National Agriculture Library Database and the Commonwealth Agriculture Bureau Database (CAB Abstracts) are helpful. The catalog of the National Library of Medicine lists health and sports medicine research studies.

HPER, not unlike anthropology and criminal justice, has not produced a full service set of reference tools. Fortunately, a few basic reference sets are readily available. Compendiums of professional sports statistics and data are essential. *The Baseball Encyclopedia*[1] is one very good example. *Baseball Trade Register*[2] is another. Similar publications are available for other sports. Annual compilations showing sports results for the year are also valuable. *Sports Market Place*[3] published by Sportsguide is a detailed directory of organizations and publications in each individual sport.

Especially notable is *Recreation and Outdoor Life Directory* published by Wasserman.[4] It covers organizations, government agencies, grants, colleges, journals, special library collections, research centers, speakers bureaus, awards, halls of fame, and festivals. Data sources whether for tourism statistics, attendance records at sporting events, or the incidence of disease are significant reference tools. Beyond the *Statistical Abstract of the United States* which is often a good starting point, the *American Statistics Index* and the *Statistical References Index* (both published by Congressional Information Service) are excellent and comprehensive sources of data.

Statistical sources from the field of health, such as hospital statistics from the American Hospital Association and *Health, United*

States, an annual publication of the federal government, can be supplemented by statistical sources from the field of business. Insurance, with interest in health, recreation, and wellness that reduce medical care costs, and sporting goods and health products industries all add to the statistical record.

As should be clear by now, the literature to the HPER field is extremely diverse and scattered. To answer any specific, complex query, effort and knowledge are required to efficiently probe this hodgepodge of material.

For those trying to build a library collection of HPER materials, a number of publications have emerged that provide bibliographies usable as selection tools. An outstanding guide has been edited by Beth J. Shapiro and John Whaley. It is *Selection of Library Materials in Applied and Interdisciplinary Fields*.[5] Two chapters are of particular importance, one on sports and recreation and the other on the health sciences. Brandon and Hill have published *Selection List of Books and Journals for the Small Medical Library*.[6] Despite its title, it has significant value for allied health collections, general academic libraries, and public libraries. It is updated periodically.

GUIDES AND LISTS

An ERIC document published in 1981 entitled *Select Guide to Health Sciences and Information*[7] provides listings of indexes and abstracts, guides and handbooks, drug information handbooks, dictionaries, statistical sources, directories, biographical sources, and both general and specialized databases. This 161 item list is a rich source of reference tools in the health fields.

Also useful is "*A Recommended Core List for Public Health Libraries*" by Kronenfeld, Watson, et al which appeared in *Medical Reference Services Quarterly*.[8] A brief article by Marian E. Kneer in the *Journal of Physical Education, Recreation and Dance*[9] highlights a few basic methods of finding information in those fields. For sport science bibliography, Jeanne Law Spala provides a guide in an article published in *Medical Reference Services Quarterly*.[10] Another bibliography of core sources is contained in *Sports and Physical Education: A Guide to Reference Resources* by Gratch, Chan, and Lingenfelter.[11] A rather different emphasis is made by

Yoko Kato in an article entitled "Materials on Sports and Games in Humanities Collections" which appeared in *Collection Building*.[12] A key literature review of recreation was published in 1986 by a presidential commission and is the first place to look for an indepth treatment of that topic.[13] All of these publications are recommended as supplements to standard sources such as *Library Journal*, *Choice*, and book reviews in journals covering those fields.

For those libraries fortunate enough to subscribe to the Research Libraries Information Network (RLIN), specific subject searches of great complexity can produce valuable bibliographies that can serve as answers to queries or as selection wish lists. RLIN, a powerful database for monographic literature, is an excellent supplement to database searching in commercial databanks. Thus in collection development activity, not unlike reference work, ready made bibliographies can help draw roadmaps of the information terrain. Together, RLIN and commercial online services for journal citations construct a super highway to quality information.

While online searching can assist the selection process, its phenomenal power lies in its ability to find precise groups of relevant citations that answer complex reference questions in a very timely fashion. Some databases are obvious places to look for information while others may seem very bizarre yet yield constructive results. ERIC, a government sponsored education database, indexes journal literature and unpublished documents in all three HPER fields in a range of areas far broader than just education.

PsycINFO and MENTAL HEALTH ABSTRACTS are much more inclusive than pure psychology and also provide significant coverage in each HPER field where those fields intersect with psychology.

SOCIOLOGICAL ABSTRACTS, on the other hand, will tend to contain less relevant information than ERIC or the psychology databases and some of the information in SOCIOLOGICAL ABSTRACTS will also be in PsycINFO.

SOCIAL SCISEARCH®, SCISEARCH®, and ARTS & HUMANITIES CITATION INDEX may provide useful citations as long as the topic is not too complex. These citation indexes find key articles that lead to other more recent articles, enabling the development of longer bibliographies.

Business databases, in particular ABI/INFORM®, PTS PROMT, and TRADE & INDUSTRY™, as well as BUSINESS DATELINE® for a local business slant, are useful sources for a range of topics such as commercial recreation, sports management, wellness and fitness programs, tourism, the hotel, motel and transportation industries amongst others.

The health field has particularly good coverage online. MEDLINE® which largely corresponds to its print counterpart, and Biological Abstracts are the most important broad based medical databases. There is also extensive health coverage in sport. Additionally, there are a number of specialized databases that are very important in the health field or have aspects of HPER embedded in them. Exclusive to BRS are AGELINE which focuses on the aging process and the elderly, and REHABDATA from the National Rehabilitation Information Center. Other useful databases include CANCERLIT®, HEALTH PLANNING & ADMINISTRATION (which combines Hospital Literature Index citations with relevant health planning material from MEDLINE®), NURSING AND ALLIED HEALTH, INTERNATIONAL PHARMACEUTICAL ABSTRACTS, SMOKING AND HEALTH (exclusive in DIALOG) and DRUG INFO (exclusive in BRS) which combines the literature on drug abuse and alcohol abuse.

The aforementioned are obvious sources for HPER material. HPER topics, however, can be found where least expected and some of these yield an abundance of useful material. The AEROSPACE DATABASE and NTIS, for example, provided a significant number of citations in response to a query concerning motor skills. CAB ABSTRACTS has an extensive subfile on recreation and tourism which is international in scope. To answer a question about the hotel industry in Zaire, articles were found in CAB as well as in FOREIGN TRADE & ECON ABSTRACTS. If one wanted to research the preference of tourists for credit cards versus travellers checks, one could find pertinent information in these two databases and in ABI/INFORM, PTS PROMT, and in SPORT. One could also look at PsycINFO and FINIS, the bank marketing association database. Some of these same databases would also provide citations to articles discussing the impact of gambling in Atlantic City on the established gambling industry in Nevada. Because this subject is site specific, local news databases such as BUSINESS DATELINE® and VUTEXT may prove very fruitful.

While SPORT and MEDLINE® are obvious places to look for articles on dehydration and fluid loss by wrestlers, BIOSIS PREVIEWS® would also be a good choice. Better design of sports equipment for the safety and health of the athlete is a subject found not only in SPORT and in MEDLINE®, but articles can also be found in COMPENDEX® PLUS, the engineering database and in DISSERTATIONS ABSTRACTS ONLINE as well.

The discussion of sources and databases should serve to emphasize that there has been a widespread diffusion of HPER topics into many areas of knowledge. The illustrative examples suggest some of the strategies needed to access information and to enhance collections in this important field.

REFERENCES

1. *The Baseball Encyclopedia*. (New York: Macmillan, 1986-).
2. *The Baseball Trade Register*. (New York: Macmillan, 1984).
3. *Sports Market Place*. (Connecticut: Grey House, 1981).
4. *Recreation and Outdoor Life Directory*. (Detroit: Gale Research Co., 1979).
5. *Selection of Library Materials in Applied and Interdisciplinary Fields*. (Chicago: American Library Association, 1987).
6. *Selection List of Books and Journals for the Small Medical Library*. (Dallas: Majors Scientific Books, Inc., 1979).
7. *Select Guide to Sources of Health Information*. Nollen, Sheila. ED 286 845.
8. "A Recommended Core Book List for Public Health Libraries." *Medical Reference Services Quarterly*, Vol. 4(2), Summer, 1985.
9. "Help! Where to Look." *JOPERD*, August 1984.
10. "Sport Science Literature." *Medical Reference Services Quarterly*, Vol. 4(2), Summer 1985.
11. *Sports and Physical Education: A Guide to Reference Resources*. (Connecticut: Greenwood Press, 1983).
12. "Materials on Sports and Games in Humanities Collections." *Collection Building*, Winter 1985.
13. *A Literature Review from the President's Commission on Americans Outdoors*. Washington, D.C., Supt. of Documents, 1987.

Legal Research Works for Non-Law Students

Bill Bailey

SUMMARY. Increasingly now non-law students—those majoring in the social sciences—want to learn more about legal research. They hear law talked about at every level in and out of the university, especially in popular culture where "mouthpiece" stories are second in prevalence only to cop stories. Non-law students discover that professors give higher grades to term papers incorporating legal issues. Such papers are more substantial as are speeches, debates, and class participation that include discussion of the law. This article encourages libraries that can afford it to build a basic law collection, and once in place, gives examples of how to teach the rudiments of law in an interesting way.

Today's university students not in pursuit of a law degree still find law an absorbing study. The entertainment industry is partly responsible. Television and film show riveting courtroom scenes in which wily adversaries—the prosecutor and the public defender—engage in verbal battle. Their ability to persuade a sour-faced jury one way or another is so masterful that we applaud, though usually the public defender is the hero or heroine and the prosecutor, the villainous inquisitor. At this writing Scott Turow's legal yarn THE BURDEN OF PROOF tops the bestsellers' list and his earlier novel, PRESUMED INNOCENT, is a major movie just out this summer. A lawyer himself, Turow recently graced the cover of TIME magazine and the large sums of money he makes from both professions tantalize students. Of course more than legal wrangling stimulates interest in fictional accounts of the legal profession.

Bill Bailey is Head of Reference, Newton Gresham Library, Sam Houston State University, Huntsville, TX 77341.

As anyone knows who has watched "L.A. Law" not only the clients but the lawyers are caught in sexual and ethical flagrante delicto. Naturally, the extra spice adds flavor to the usual dull food of the lawyer's life. But real-life lawyers generate excitement too. Take for example Gerry Spence, Imelda Marcos' savior, or any of the many corporate lawyers who pocket six-figure salaries. These advocates inspire a sense of wonder and invincibility, so much so that students stand in awe of the law. Yet at the same time they want to taste for themselves the heady elixir of jurisprudence.

Having a complete law collection in general reference is an obvious luxury due to the expense. Many libraries shelve what incomplete law materials they have in three places: some in government documents, some in the stacks, and the remainder in reference. I recommend pulling it together and making it a discrete part of general reference, i.e., a separate collection not far removed. If your library can afford to buy the entire NATIONAL REPORTER SYSTEM and the GENERAL DIGEST it should. This purchase gives your students access to most every case decided in U.S. courts at the appellate level or above. A not-inexpensive set of SHEPARD'S CITATIONS will update the cases for you.

Add the U.S. CODE ANNOTATED for federal statutes and your state statutes along with several law dictionaries and you have an integrated law collection. It will become so popular you will need one last item—the LSAT study guide. Since the purpose of this article is to look at the bright side of reference service, I will cease and desist from collection building and talk about the pleasures of legal reference work.

JOYS OF LEGAL WORK

Jane Roe et al., Appellants v. *Henry Wade*, 410 U.S. 113, 93 S.Ct., 705, 35 L.Ed.2d 147, is a case very familiar in name to most students. But do they really know much about *Roe* v. *Wade* other than it is a landmark case concerning abortion? This is where the librarian steps in to deliver a lecture. *Roe* v. *Wade* offers a perfect example of what is referred to as case law. Few non-law students have heard of this concept though find it intriguing once explained. As defined by BLACK'S LAW DICTIONARY, case law is "the aggregate of reported cases as forming a body of jurisprudence, or the law of a particular subject as evidenced or formed by the adjudged cases, in distinction to statutes, regulations, and other sources of law—see Common law." Therefore the first step in clarifying case law for students and in turn *Roe* v. *Wade* is to cut through the legalese. Once you decipher BLACK'S—that case law is unlegislated law that carries the same weight as that legislated—students begin to see the light. A hand shoots up with a question, "Then there are no legislated abortion laws in effect?" You reply, yes and no.

Each state has legislated its own abortion laws relative to such things as parental consent, a doctor's right to refuse to perform an abortion, what constitutes a viable fetus, and so on. But the basis for the current statutes comes from the case law established in *Roe* v. *Wade* when in 1973 the U.S. Supreme Court established the trimester rule: any woman or the State on behalf of the woman can ask for and expect to obtain an abortion within the first three months of pregnancy; after that the State has the sole right to regulate or forbid abortion except when it is necessary to preserve the mother's health. "What was the law before *Roe* v. *Wade*?" Dismal.

In Texas where Jane Roe went to court the Penal Code statutes—not case law—prior to 1973 were explicit: two to five years in prison for any one performing an abortion; if done without the woman's consent double the punishment; any procurer of the abortion is equally guilty; if the abortion attempt fails a fine of $100 to $1,000 shall be paid to the State; if the mother dies it is the same as murder; and in a final stricter passage, destroying an unborn child is punishable by five years to life imprisonment. Statutory law exacts punishment; case law doesn't.

While elaborating this to students, the difference between statutory and case law becomes much clearer. But to really get their attention you must tell the human side of the story. Jane Roe, an unmarried woman, got pregnant in 1970 and wanted a safe abortion performed in a hospital by a licensed physician, not a quack job done in a seedy motel room. Roe didn't want to bear a child out of wedlock, alone and financially strapped, nor did she want to raise a child under the onus of illegitimacy. Living in Dallas County, Texas she was told abortions were illegal in the state. So "on behalf of herself and all other women" she decided to contest the unjust law.

Dr. James Hubert Hallford joined Roe in her fight. He contended the state statutes were vague and uncertain and violated the Fourteenth Amendment, privacy rights, and his right to practice medicine. A married couple, John and Mary Doe, also initiated a suit against the State alleging that an unwanted pregnancy would worsen a neural-chemical disorder afflicting Mrs. Doe. The three disputants aimed their complaints at Henry Wade, the county district attorney. But all didn't go well.

Dr. Hallford lost his plea early on; he already faced two criminal charges for having performed illegal abortions so his testimony was tainted by prior action. Likewise the Does had to leave the courtroom losers; they based their complaint on a future condition and appeared more interested in selfishly avoiding children at any cost than in protecting Mrs. Doe's delicate health. Jane Roe, however, won the trimester rule for all women.

There is so much in the case to interest students: a history of abortion laws from ancient times to the present, the position of the American Medical Association and the American Public Health Association on abortion, and finally Justice Rehnquist's dissenting opinion. Rehnquist's nay-saying alone can generate a solid thirty minutes to an hour of heated discussion. Mainly, he holds that because a majority of states have restricted abortion for at least a century—demonstrating a prudent consensus—the law should remain unchanged. So in class you drum up a pitched battle between law and women's liberation, between male-rendered statutes and freedom of choice, and between law overstepping its bounds and a woman's control of her own body.

LIGHTER CASES

On the lighter side, a case such as *Lisa Litchfield, Plaintiff-Appellant* v. *Steven Spielberg* et al., 736 F2d 1352, causes students to laugh out loud and underscores a fundamental aspect of American jurisprudence: anyone with a legal complaint has the right to be heard in a court of law. Before reading Litchfield's accusation, I instruct the class it will be the sole jury in this matter. Each class-member must believe beyond a shadow of a doubt in the guilt or innocence of Spielberg. His career as a successful moviemaker hangs in the balance. Whereas if Lisa Litchfield is correct she should receive full and immediate compensation for Spielberg's ill treatment of her. Here are the particulars of the case.

In 1978 Litchfield wrote a one-act play entitled "Lokey from Maldemar" followed by public performances. After which Litchfield submitted "Lokey" to the defendant Universal City Studios, Inc. in the hope a movie would be made of it. In 1979 Universal rejected "Lokey" but Litchfield continued to show it to other Hollywood studios without any luck. On June 11, 1982 the defendants' film "E.T. — The Extraterrestrial" opened nationwide and became the most successful movie of the 1980s. Litchfield claims the defendants pirated "Lokey" and she should receive full credit for its conception and the money due her as author. I now read from the case transcript:

> As originally developed in 1978, 'Lokey' was a musical play about the adventures of two aliens, Fudinkle and Lokey, who are temporarily stranded on Earth when their spacecraft is immobilized by gravity. After landing near the North Pole, the aliens meet Lisa Marie, her younger brother Michael, and their father, a scientist stationed at the Sorenson Research Center at the North Pole. After temporarily detaining the children with an energy field, the aliens quickly learn English and are invited home by Lisa Marie to meet her father. At the cabin, Lokey demonstrates his extraordinary extraterrestrial powers by psychokinetically taking a gun away from her father; reviving the father from a heart attack; projecting a map of the Earth on the cabin wall through mind power; and revealing his own destiny as a future ruler of his planet. Lisa Marie demonstrates her own terrestrial charms, teaching Lokey to kiss and inducing him to promise to send 'mind pictures' to her after the aliens' departure. Fudinkle and Lokey then travel to a beach in Japan, where they capsize a fishing boat filled with porpoise hunters. Next, the aliens travel to the Andes Mountains, where they meet Tollie Marx, a prophetic witch. Finally, all of the characters appear on the edge of the Pacific

Ocean, where the aliens bid the humans farewell as they return to their ship.

Needless-to-say, students having seen "E.T." and that is usually all of them get a real kick out of this fanciful law case. To no one's surprise Spielberg et al. won. As the laughter dies down, I center in-class discussion around what constitutes a legitimate case of law and why American courts are so overcrowded due to unwarranted complaints like Litchfield's.

SPIDER WEBS

By the time students reach college they have heard about the spider web of federal regulations that won't let any infraction escape. A decade before Ronald Reagan's rash experiments in deregulation, a librarian could have said the CODE OF FEDERAL REGULATIONS represents government control at its worst. The multi-volume set seemingly contained dos and don'ts for everything. But now that Americans are wiser and have seen the aftermath of deregulation—the airline industry's poorer safety record and the savings & loan fiasco for starters—the CODE OF FEDERAL REGULATIONS doesn't look so bureaucratic. Maybe it should be double the size! Whether that is advisable or not engenders instantaneous debate. I point out to students that Telecommunications, Title 47, is five volumes long or 2,898 pages. And that Protection of the Environment, Title 40, runs through fourteen volumes or 10,265 pages. I try to redeem ex-President Reagan by saying he got a bum rap when called a foe of environmental protection since clearly a forest of federal regulations exists. I need say no more because hands wave at me as if everyone in class were drowning. "But Reagan didn't enforce the regulations," they all reply. "What good is law if no one makes polluters act right?" There before my eyes I see a sudden loss of innocence and murmur to myself—welcome to the world.

Another favorite of mine to wow students with is to show them the 1948 edition of VERNON'S TEXAS STATUTES. Volume I, the Revised Civil Statutes & Rules of Civil Procedure, contains 2,447 pages; Volume II, the Penal Code & Code of Criminal Procedure, 1,724 pages. To be sure two thick volumes but nothing compared to today's 125 volumes of VERNON'S and who knows how many pages. The General Index alone is 2,739 pages—larger than Volume I of the 1948 edition. Other states' statutes have a similar history. Why such an increase in legal strictures, I ask? To protect us better and because new areas of law crop up all the time. My glib justification for a greatly expanded Ten Commandments doesn't satisfy one student. He responds, "Too many idle lawyers." Actually more laws are advantageous, I try to explain. Sharper definition of the law reduces shady interpretation. People who want to circumvent the law can always find a way if the law isn't encompassing. Here after working so hard to win student confidence with *Roe* v. *Wade*, the *Spielberg* case, and a look at excessive but necessary federal regulations, I meet my Waterloo. Students naturally hate laws pinned on everything. They had rather go their own way unfettered by prohibition—not yet realizing that absolute freedom in life is a chimera.

So in a last ditch effort to win them back I pull out my secret weapon: legal forms. Three of the most popular student requests for legal aid are in the areas of tenant-landlord relations, forming a partnership, and divorce. We have a campus lawyer whose office is in the counseling center; it is her job to give students legal advice. But being a curious lot students come to the library wanting to do their own legal research. That's fine; that's one reason why we spend a bundle on law books. When I open the pages to a divorce form and a nervous student sees a fill-in-the-blank exit visa, I've done my job. All I can add is study the form or forms depending on your particular situation and then call a lawyer. Sometimes I conclude with it's your right to act as your own lawyer, but be very careful if you choose to file a legal document without benefit of counsel. You may encounter judicial resistance. Then like an apparition I disappear before the devil of malpractice spears me. Legal forms fascinate students who think before seeing them that lawyers handwrite their documents by candlelight way beyond midnight. Therefore, a fee of $500 is little enough for all their work. But having a secretary key in information on a computerized form, taking all of ten minutes to complete it, is a "rip-off"—no, "good work, if you can get it."

What I have related so far about legal research for non-law students has involved my in-class attempts to demystify law. I will end with a poignant anecdote that to this day jumps to mind when I recall the many queries I've heard in more than a decade of legal reference work. A young male student noticeably flustered asked where the law books were. Not wanting to point and send him to flounder, I took him to the law stacks. Once there he told me his purpose. He wanted to know what statutory rape was in the eyes of the law. I found a cite in the index and handed him the appropriate volume to read. Back at the reference desk, I awaited the next patron. A few minutes later that patron was the same red-faced young man who I knew a bit more about this time. He placed the law book in front of me and pleaded, "What does this mean? I don't understand it very well." I'm sorry, I said, I can't interpret law for you because I'm not a lawyer. "But you've got to help me. I can't ask anybody else. And I need to know right away." I could see the student ached inside, so I glanced at the text. This is really very clear, I said. Why don't you read it one more time. "Oh, I understand about the age of the girl and whether she consent to it or not it's still . . . you know . . . but my girl and I are going to get married." Then what is your question? "Well, it's not clear—the crime. I mean it, the law, only covers one time—just once. What if you did it over and over again?" The poor boy must have envisioned fifty gallows.

Scholarly Communication, Peer Review, and Reference Librarian Ethics: A Case Study of the *Lexicon of the Middle Ages*

Gordon Moran

SUMMARY. There is some apparent conflict involving reference librarian ethics and their relationship to some recently published views relating to peer review and the scholarly communication system. A case study, based on the gap between the promotional rhetoric and the actual peer review, editorial practices of a famous reference work, the *Lexicon of the Middle Ages* (Artemis Verlag, Munich), brings this conflict into sharp relief.

An academic debate in the field of art history of the Middle Ages, known as the Guide Riccio controversy, has been called the "case of the century" in art history. Material distributed by the *Lexicon of the Middle Ages* states that in the case of controversies, protagonists of opposing sides will have the chance to express their ideas in the pages of the lexicon. But the protagonists of one side of the Guide Riccio controversy were flatly rejected. If providing accurate information, and providing access to all sides of an issue, are tenets of library ethics, it would seem logical that academic and reference librarians would become professional allies of the academic whistleblower.

This case study is, to some extent, a discussion of how some established tenets of library ethics and reference librarian ethics seem to have come into direct conflict with some recently expressed views about scholarly communication. In an age of a so-called information explosion, should scholars have access, in academic libraries, to all sides of a scholarly debate, or should recognized peer

---

Gordon Moran is an independent scholar, Via delle Terme, 3, Firenze, Italy.

© 1991 by The Haworth Press, Inc. All rights reserved.

review authorities determine which ideas in a scholarly debate should be allowed to be communicated to scholars via academic libraries?

The Summer of 1982 issue of *The Reference Librarian* is devoted to "Ethics and Reference Services." In it, the following is written:

> Information provided the user in response to an inquiry must be the most accurate possible.[1]

> ... it is our duty to provide more information ... by promoting discussion and insuring that the widest range of information and ideas possible are available.[2]

> ... there is also the need to alert and show users how to avoid the rip-off type of biographical dictionaries, old encyclopedias in new covers and other fraudulent ventures all of us are exposed to.[3]

In terms of the academic library, these ethical considerations indicate that the reference librarian should give the scholar information that is as accurate and as complete as possible, and also that the reference librarian should alert scholars to deficiencies in specific reference works.

The three passages cited above, written by librarians, are in keeping with the tenets of academic ethics on a broader level, which affirm that the pursuit of truth is the foundation of academic ethics. In this regard, Ernst Nolte writes, "The first requirement of the academic ethic is the obligation of methodically striving for the truth."[4] Likewise, Walter Rüegg affirms that "the absolute commandment of respect for the truth is fundamental to the exercise of scientific and scholarly professions."[5] Since the search for the truth often turns out to be a complex and elusive process, it would seem logical that "accurate" information and the "widest range of information and ideas possible" would be both helpful and essential.

At the same time, the academic library is regarded by some scholars as a link, or as a subordinate part, in a larger system known as "scholarly communication." For example, Charles Osburn, an academic librarian, states the following: "We have discovered our place in what is now called the scholarly communication system ... authorities in a given field determine the validity and assess the relative significance of a particular contribution of a scholar or scientist within that field ... The relative importance of a given output of scholarly communication is determined through its acceptance or rejection by the recognized peer review authority in each field."[6] Osburn's views lead to the question of whether academic librarians should give scholars access to "given output of scholarly communication" (facts, ideas, theories, new information, etc.) which the "recognized" peer review authorities have flatly rejected. (Or, in other words, should the academic librarian treat the academic whistleblower in the same way that the peer review authorities do?) Osburn takes the stand that the academic librarians' role is to carry out the decisions of the peer review authorities. Along this line, he writes that changing the "role" of the library in the scholarly communication system will end up "rendering the system of scholarly communication incomprehensible and very incoherent."[7] Inasmuch as the contents of many reference works available in academic libraries have been edited, directed, compiled, and written by recognized peer review authorities, it would seem that Osburn's ideas are especially pertinent for the reference librarian.

PEER REVIEW

At the same time, however, the subjects of peer review and peer review authority have also themselves become recent topics of study. For instance, in 1985 the Office of Scholarly Communication of ACLS conducted a survey in which nearly 4,000 scholars responded. In a discussion of the results of this survey, the following is written: "About three out of four respondents think the editorial peer review system is biased ... About 40 percent think bias is so prevalent in their disciplines that it merits reform.... The question is, therefore, not whether bias exists in the peer review system, but whether it is prevalent and whether it systematically interferes with the free exchange of information and ideas by discriminating against particular subjects, opinions, and classes of authors.... The survey shows that suspicions of bias appear to be held by scholars in all types of universities and among all the disciplines sampled ... the unease is pervasive, not an occasional outcropping of discontent."[8] Nor is peer review bias and suppression anything new in academia. The clamorous case of how recognized peer review authorities treated the discovery (the cause of childbirth fever) of Ignazio Semmelweis, and of how they obstinately refused to correct their peer review errors, took place more than a century ago.

At this point, it can be imagined that peer review bias and suppression might well affect the contents of reference works. It would also seem to follow that, in terms of effective use of a specific reference work, the reference librarian's ability to give "accurate" information, and to give "the widest range of information and ideas possible" would be hindered to the extent that specific accurate information (and unwanted, embarrassing ideas) had been rejected, suppressed, and censored by peer review authorities from the text of the reference work. To the extent that this happens, therefore, peer review authorities would be in effect hampering reference librarians from carrying out their ethical obligations of providing scholars with access to accurate information and access to all sides of an academic controversy. (The argument that specific peer review bias, errors, and malpractice might experience self-correction sometime in the future does not help the reference librarian who is asked to give the information *before* such hypothetical corrections are made at some time in the vague future.)

Such problems could be alleviated, to a degree, if the editors, directors, compilers, and authors of academic reference works made it a point to include in the texts all sides of scholarly controversial issues and academic debates. The promotional literature of some reference works claims to do just that, directly or indirectly. If the reality does not live up to the promotional rhetoric, however, both the reference librarian and the scholar might be misled. For example, if in the face of such rhetoric a controversial issue is discussed in the text without comment about the controversy surrounding the issue, the reader might assume that no controversy exists. Out of cite, out of mind.

A CASE STUDY

Some time ago (January 1988) I received an unsolicited request from the *Lexicon of the Middle Ages* (Artemis Verlag, Munich) to write an article in art history for the pages of their reference work.

Specifically, the topic was "Domenico Ghirlandaio" (a Florentine painter of the second half of the 15th century). I am not a specialist in this field of study. To the contrary, my art history studies are predominantly in the field of 14th century Sienese painting, and large parts of these studies have been conducted in collaboration with Michael Mallory (Art Department, Brooklyn College of CUNY), who is also a specialist in 14th century Sienese painting.

At any rate, enclosed along with the request (and contract) to write about Ghirlandaio was various promotional and explanatory material which described the lexicon and its editorial policies. Among this material, the following is written: "A great many people are interested in acquiring as much reliable and detailed information as possible about the period and gaining an insight into the mentality and the way of life.". . . . "It is invaluable . . . for all scholars doing research into . . . the history of art." . . . ". . . a reference work which for the first time presents all the available knowledge on the European Middle Ages on a scholarly basis in a lucid and generally understandable form. Its primary aim is *absolutely reliable information expressed as concisely as possible.*" . . . . ". . . reflects the results of the latest research into the Middle Ages. In the case of controversial problems and theories the Lexicon also gives the protagonists of opposing positions a chance to express their views without academic polemics. What is disputed must be described as controversial or uncertain." A promotional brochure also claims that this lexicon "has long since been accepted internationally as . . . the greatest encyclopaedic achievement of the twentieth century."

THE GUIDO RICCIO CONTROVERSY

Volume II of the *Lexicon of the Middle Ages* was published in 1983, and Volume III in 1986. In 1977 a controversy in the history of art began, and since then has been consistently intensifying, particularly after 1980. This academic debate, known as the Guido Riccio controversy, has been called the "case of the century" in art history. Some passages from Alice Wohl's account (from an article written in 1984, with the specific title "The Case of The Century") give an idea of the intensity of the debate: "A startling discovery . . . one of the most famous paintings in the world . . . The ensuing controversy has shocked and divided the community of art scholars and has set the Italian press in an uproar. . . . The image is renowned both as a masterpiece of late medieval painting and as a symbol of Siena's history . . . It is considered a cornerstone of Simone's art as well as the origin of heroic equestrian portraiture . . . Headlines in the local papers—and later in national ones—announced the challenge. . . . Speculation was intense. . . . Hotly disagreeing with the theory that the recently uncovered fresco is the real Guidoriccio by Simone . . . The controversy centerstage. . . . If this is the case, then art history will have to be rewritten. . . . The 'case of the century' is far from closed."[9]

Other authors have also commented on the controversial nature of the Guido Riccio studies. The selected excerpts that follow give further evidence that this academic debate and scholarly controversy is being very keenly contested:

> The hottest issue in art history today involves a time-honored symbol of Italian Renaissance art. . . . Now at the center of attention in a controversy that has shaken the art history world, the fresco must be viewed in a new light . . . Affirmations, accusations, denials, claims and counterclaims will continue to fly from one camp to the other in this art history war until the riddle is solved. (Jane Fogarty)[10]

> This is the latest and most controversial twist in a saga that has been dividing art scholars for months and has been dubbed 'the case of the century.' (Peter Watson)[11]

> This fresco, long attributed to Simone Martini, has lately been the subject of much controversy, for its former provenance has crumbled beneath the weight of serious scrutiny, sending tremors through the ranks of art historians. (Anne Marshall Zwack)[12]

> . . . the shock waves are reverberating harder than ever. . . . The picture . . . was one of Simone's most famous—one reproduced constantly in art-history textbooks dealing with the period. . . . It has adorned the jacket of more than one art-history text. . . . His first doubts threatened to tarnish the reputations of many art historians. . . . The controversy has exploded . . . (William Raynor)[13]

> Controversy in Siena. . . . For the last nine years there has been growing disagreement about who painted Siena's most famous fresco. . . . a growing crescendo of comment in both the Italian and the international media. The issue has developed into one of the great art historical questions of the century . . . (Richard Fremantle)[14]
>
> . . . his inquiries would touch off one of the most intense and acrimonious battles in the annals of art history. In the 12 years that have elapsed since the fresco's authenticity was first challenged, the controversy over who painted it has split specialists into opposing camps. (Jane Boutwell)[15]
>
> The controversy . . . turned into an animated diatribe that has not yet been placated. . . . How disorienting . . . when learned art historians contradict one another so drastically . . . (Cecilia Jannella)[16]

In short, what generations of students and scholars had been taught and led to believe as true might be, instead, very false. Without going into details of a scholarly nature, Prof. Michael Mallory and I have accumulated more than fifty reasons (of a technical, historical, iconographical, stylistic nature) to doubt the traditional textbook-encyclopedia position on the subject. It seems difficult to imagine a greater controversy regarding a specific academic debate about the Middle Ages.

Therefore, having read the notice that "In the case of controversial problems and theories the Lexicon also gives the protagonists of opposing positions a chance to express their views . . . ," I informed an official of the editorial board, Gloria Avella-Widhalm, of the Guido Riccio controversy, and requested permission to write a short article, expressing our new findings and theories, for inclusion in the *Lexicon of the Middle Ages*. I reminded Avella-Widhalm about the editorial policy statement that in the case of controversies all sides have the opportunity to have their views expressed in the pages of the lexicon. (At the same time, I declined the offer to write an art history article on Domenico Ghirlandaio, since I am not a specialist on the subject. I also requested permission to write a short article on the Beato Ambrogio controversy in Medieval religious history, for which I am an author.)

STONEWALLING?

My requests, written on January 26, 1988, were not acknowledged nor answered. Therefore, on March 18, 1988, I wrote a follow-up letter in which I reminded Avella-Widhalm once again about the editorial policy regarding controversial issues. I also mentioned that one of the lexicon's own scholar/advisors is Prof. Walter Rüegg, who had written in 1986 (in the article cited above in *Minerva*) that "the absolute commandment of respect for the truth is fundamental" for academic ethics. Meanwhile, on January 27, I also wrote to Rüegg about his *Minerva* article, in relation to my studies of academic ethics and peer review. When no acknowledgement nor reply was received from him, on February 27 I wrote a follow-up letter to him. In this letter I pointed out to him the apparent "stonewalling" that was seemingly taking place on the part of the editorial board of the *Lexicon of the Middle Ages*, as far as the request to write an article on the Guido Riccio controversy was concerned. I also asked, "Does the academic 'commandment of respect for the truth' apply to the editorial policy of the 'Lexikon' and to the contents of the 'Lexikon'?"

At this point, in a letter of March 25, the lexicon editorial board member, Gloria Avella-Widhalm, replied negatively to the request to express our views regarding the Guido Riccio controversy. Essentially, three reasons were given to justify this rejection:

1. There is not enough room in the lexicon for our views on the Guido Riccio controversy.
2. Her knowledge of the subject indicates that the traditional scholarly view is the prevailing view in the literature in this field of study.
3. Guido Riccio is an art history topic, while the lexicon deals with all aspects of the Middle Ages, of which art history is just one of several. Avella-Widhalm then suggested that we should take our proposed article to a more specialized reference work, such as the *Enciclopedia dell'arte medievale*.

(In a letter dated April 1, Walter Rüegg supports the rejection decision. His reasons for rejection follow, rather closely, those of Avella-Widhalm.)

I think these reasons for rejection merit comment and analysis, in terms of whether or not the promotional and explanatory literature of the lexicon might be misleading and deceiving reference librarians (and reviewers of reference works) as far as "reliable" and accurate information is concerned. First of all, if there is not room in the lexicon for our point of view on the Guido Riccio controversy, why do the editors write, "In the case of controversial problems and theories the lexicon also gives the protagonists of opposing positions a chance to express their views . . . ?" Secondly, if our "views" could not be expressed in the lexicon because they were not the prevalent views found in the scholarly literature on the subject, it would be more truthful on the part of the editors of the lexicon to state that in the case of controversies the lexicon will not necessarily give space to the protagonists who challenge the traditional and prevalent views in the literature on the subject.

Furthermore, if the Guido Riccio controversy cannot be included because it is a subject in the field of art history, why did an editorial board member request a scholar who is a protagonist in the Guido Riccio controversy to write an article on Domenico Ghirlandaio, which is also a topic in the field of art history? Besides, why should a prolonged controversy that has been described as "the case of the century" and the "enigma of the century" in art history be excluded — specifically on the basis that it is an art history subject —, at the very same time that the promotional literature proudly proclaims that the lexicon is "invaluable" as a reference work for "all scholars doing research into . . . the history of art?" Moreover, the request by a protagonist in the Beato Ambrogio controversy to have his views expressed was also rejected.

At this point, the reference librarian might ask, "What controversies are actually referred to in the statement "In the case of controversial problems and theories the Lexicon also gives the protagonists of opposing positions a chance to express their views . . . ?" If the Guido Riccio controversy is rejected because it is in the field of art history of the Middle Ages, why would controversies in political history, history of science, history of music, religion, etc. be allowed? Obviously, there are few—if any—academic controversies, or academic debates, in studies of the Middle Ages that are not part of some academic discipline or field of study, so why should art history (and religious history, for that matter) be suddenly singled out for exclusion as far as scholarly controversies are concerned? In this case, it would seem that Avella-Widhalm, Rüegg, and others on the editorial and advisory boards, would either have to claim that a controversy does not exist regarding Guido Riccio, or they must admit that they made a false statement when it was written that in the cases of controversies the protagonists of opposing sides would have a chance to express their views. But in order to claim that a Guido Riccio controversy does not exist, they would have to deny the truth and validity of the statements of the observers who have followed the debate closely, and they would also have to deny the contents—and the very existence—of the extensive literature on the subject. With such a denial, however, it would seem that Prof. Rüegg would be placed in the position of either retracting his published statements about commitment to truth, or else claiming that, for some reason, the *Lexicon of the Middle Ages* does not have to live up to that commitment in its totality.

The facts and discussion in this case study indicate that there is a gap between the promotional rhetoric and the actual specific editorial practices of the reference work in question. It can be doubted that this case is an isolated one as far as reference works are concerned. In fact, if the results of the 1985 ACLS survey (cited above) are any indication, it seems quite possible that some other uncomfortable, upsetting, and otherwise unwanted scholarly ideas might have been suppressed and censored from the pages of the *Lexicon of the Middle Ages*, and from the pages of every other similar reference work as well. Obviously, this is a situation that is virtually impossible to quantify with precision. Wilfred Cude considers the problem of academic suppression to be a very serious one, as he writes, "In the name of collegiality, students are victimized, considerable intellectual resources are being squandered, and the general public is deliberately misled. Worse yet, the free pursuit of knowledge is itself threatened: useful information is altered or nullified, valuable arguments are suppressed, and highly-respected institutions are manipulated to serve meanly personal ends. We cannot convincingly pretend this sort of thing isn't occurring on a dismaying scale, and we only harm ourselves professionally by refusing to address the difficulties openly and vigorously."[17]

"COMPUTER VIRUS"

There have been some recent highly publicized cases of so-called "computer virus" that have affected communication systems. In such instances, certain information that was originally intended to be included in the system has been eliminated (and thus suppressed and excluded) and other information has been inserted in its place, changing the information program from that which was originally intended. If truth is the intended subject matter of the program of the scholarly communication system, it would follow that any suppression of the truth (in terms of subject matter in a scholarly discipline) and perpetuation of falsity within the system would, in effect, amount to a form of intellectual virus within the material of the academic library and its reference works.

What should the academic librarian, the reference librarian, and the reviewer of reference works do when they detect symptoms of such a virus within the contents of their library material? James Rettig maintains that the reviewer of a reference work has an "obligation" to bring such problems "to light" when they are uncovered.[18] By doing so, however, it should be kept in mind that such a "cure" for intellectual virus is unacceptable medicine in the eyes of Dr. Osburn. As mentioned, Charles Osburn believes that the recognized peer review authorities in a given discipline should have the power to determine what material is accepted or rejected, and that the "library does not and should not lead the system of scholarly communication."[19]

This question of whether or not the library and the academic librarian should "lead" the system leads directly to the related subject of the librarians' commitment to giving accurate and reliable information, and also commitment to providing access to the widest range of information and ideas on a given subject. These considerations, in turn, bring up the question of the academic librarian's view of—and treatment of—academic whistleblowers. How did the academic librarians of the day treat the works and ideas of Semmelweis during his long battle with the peer review authorities over the cause and prevention of the deadly childbirth fever that was killing so many women soon after they gave birth? How did the academic librarians, at the University of Caracas and elsewhere, treat the works and ideas of Beauperthuy, whose theories about the transmission of Yellow Fever—rejected wholesale by peer review authorities in many instances—were later proven to be valid?

Based on their writings and actions, it seems obvious that many peer review authorities, along with Osburn, regard academic whistleblowers on an adversarial basis. Do academic librarians and reference librarians regard academic whistleblowers in the same way?

As the term is generally understood, the academic whistleblower is a scholar who believes to have discovered errors of one type or another in the so-called "core" literature of a scholarly discipline, and attempts to correct these errors within the scholarly communication system. Basically, within the scholarly communication system there are two possible points of entry into the mainstream: (1) Peer review publications, including scholarly journals, books, scholarly conferences with published "Acts" or proceedings of the conferences, reference works, etc.; (2) The academic library and research library, via publications that give access to the ideas that the recognized peer review authorities had previously rejected. Such publications might include newspapers, news magazines, so-called "underground" publications, so-called "minor" publications, etc.

At the peer review level, the large, ponderous specialized encyclopedia, or similar academic reference work, sometimes attains a particular aura of authority, insofar as it is regarded as the collective wisdom and knowledge of the brightest and most erudite minds in the field. And the lists of famous scholars who appear on the editorial and advisory boards of such reference works provide effective window dressing that adds lustre to the image of authority and erudition. On the other hand, no matter who it is who is involved in peer review suppression, acts of peer review censorship and suppression should arouse suspicions among academic librarians that the truth is being covered up. In response to exposure of peer review censorship and suppression, it would seem logical that academic librarians, reference librarians, and reviewers of reference works would become natural professional allies of the academic whistleblower, since the librarian is committed, by ethical principle, to combat censorship, while the academic whistleblower is engaged in actual combat against censorship.

LET MY PEOPLE KNOW

Of course, academic librarians cannot be expected to be able to judge true from false among all the scholarly material in the library, much of which is highly specialized and technical. Such a situation might lead to a "hands off" policy among librarians (or a "hands up" policy if the librarian is confronted by much higher academic authorities on campus in an academic dispute). At the same time, librarians are, according to their own rhetoric, keen and conscientious guardians against suppression of information. In some cases at least, the lack of expertise in a given subject should not necessarily preclude the academic and reference librarian from being aware that peer review censorship and suppression of the truth has taken place.

If eternal vigilance is the price of political freedom, the librarian's vigilance against academic suppression can serve as a safeguard for intellectual freedom and academic freedom. Rettig writes that the problem of peer review suppression "ought to be solved at its roots."[20] In this regard, if a famous political motto is "Let my people go!", the librarian's appropriate ethical response to peer review censorship might be LET MY PEOPLE KNOW!

REFERENCES

1. Joan Meador, Craig Buthod, "Triage," *The Reference Librarian*, Summer, 1982, p.144.
2. Emmett Davis, "The Ethics of Information Serving Homo Sapiens vs. Homo Biblios," *The Reference Librarian*, Summer, 1982, p. 40.
3. John Lubans, Jr., "Teaching the User: Ethical Considerations," *The Reference Librarian*, Summer, 1982, p.95.
4. Ernst Nolte, "Thoughts on the State and Prospects of the Academic Ethic in the Universities of the Federal Republic of Germany," *Minerva*, Summer-Autumn, 1983, p.161.
5. Walter Rüegg, "The Academic Ethos," *Minerva*, Winter 1986, p.408.
6. Charles B. Osburn, "The Structuring of the Scholarly Communication System," *College and Research Libraries*, May, 1989, pp. 277, 279, 281.

7. Charles B. Osburn, in a letter dated October 31, 1989, to Gordon Moran.
8. Herbert C. Morton, Anne J. Price, *The ACLS Survey of Scholars*, (Lanham, Maryland: University Press of America, Inc., 1989), pp. 7-9.
9. Alice Sedwick Wohl, "The Case of the Century," *Art and Antiques*, October, 1984, pp. 68-73.
10. Jane Fogarty, "Gordon Moran and The Siege of Siena," *Florenscape*, May 15, 1987, p.25.
11. Peter Watson, "The well-shaken Martini." *The Observer*. April 20, 1986, p.21.
12. Anne Marshall Zwack, "Siena," *Gourmet*, February, 1987, p.58.
13. William Raynor, "The Case Against Simone," *Connoisseur*, October, 1984, pp. 60-62.
14. Richard Fremantle, "Moran's Martini," *Taxi*, April, 1987, pp.129-130.
15. Jane Boutwell, "Fiasco al Fresco," *Domino*, March, 1989, p.131.
16. Cecilia Jannella, *Simone Martini*, (Florence, Italy: Scala, 1989), p.63.
17. Wilfred Cude, in a letter of April 15, 1988. Cude is the author of several works on academic ethics, including; "On the Suppression of Thought by our Academics: A Presentation," *Journal of Canadian Fiction*, Fall, 1986, pp.9-43; and, *The Ph.D. Trap*, (West Bay, Nova Scotia: Medicine Label Press, 1987).
18. James Rettig, in a letter of March 16, 1989, to Gordon Moran.
19. Charles B. Osburn, in the letter of October 31, 1989.
20. James Rettig, in the letter of March 16, 1989.

III. THE PUBLIC SERVED

The International Ideology of Library and Information Science: The Past Three Decades

Stephen Karetzky

SUMMARY. The essential elements of the Anglo-American ideology of international library and information science have been stable for the past thirty years. The approach stresses the significance of "integrating" information on a global scale while restructuring existing communication channels to decrease Western power. It is held that an internationalized profession can play a vital role in the attainment of world peace, justice, and understanding.

The tenets of Western international and comparative library and information science, which are largely of American and British origin, have remained remarkably consistent for at least the past three decades. While there is some diversity of opinion on some points, there is a high degree of agreement on the major theses among those active in this area of the profession.

Perhaps the most significant belief among leaders of this field is that we now live in a "global village" in which the various nations must cooperate and unite. Many believe that library and information workers can be instrumental in realizing the dream of One World because our field itself is international, *in posse* if not *in esse*. Thus, John F. Harvey has commented on "the one world philosophy permeating this field,"[1] and Lester Asheim has written of "the hoped-for One World of Librarianship."[2] To B. C. Vickery and A. G. Brown, international cooperation and "one world of information" are inevitable: "As information science continues to develop, so also will international cooperation, for . . . information science, both in its theoretical base and its practical applications, is essentially international in character."[3]

In the preface to their landmark *Encyclopedia of Library and Information Science*, editors Allen Kent and Harold Lancour state that they are committed to building a new discipline — an integrated library and information science — and that they "are equally committed to a 'one-world' concept of their science."[4] (Their goal was to produce a work which was "non-natural.") Sylva Simsova maintains that "internationalism is a natural outcome of life in a global village in which neighbors of different cultures learn to live with one another."[5] She holds that "international understanding, which has often been given as one of the objectives of comparative librarianship, will follow as mutual understanding reduced any areas of friction."[6] Others are even more optimistic: Richard Kryzs and Gaston Litton predict that extraterrestrial librarianship will someday supersede global librarianship.[7]

D. J. Foskett asserts that all humans will perish unless ignorance and mistrust give way to knowledge and understanding. Since librarians hold key positions in the international communications network, through our cooperation and mutual assistance in librarianship "we make a genuine contribution to the achievement of peace and happiness for all men across the world."[8] The librarian Louis Shores believes that "our professional destiny is to lead this troubled world out of its current dilemmas by teaching people everywhere to compare their ideals and their societies."⁹ Libraries could become centers for fact-based dialogues on issues of war, peace, trade, and education, and also help develop a world culture that focuses on the advancement of humankind.

Closely connected with the concepts of One World and international cooperation is the idea of The Integration and Internationalization of Knowledge and Information. By supporting the "universality and integration of knowledge," Robert Vosper holds, we would help heal the world's wounds, a world divided by ideological, linguistic, political and religious differences.[10] "Perhaps the universal language of the future will be MARC!"[11] he remarks. Vosper reminds us that the dream of universal bibliographic control is an old one for librarians, citing Konrad von Gesner's sixteenth century *Biblioteca Universalis*.

Information scientists such as H. J. Abraham Goodman, Manfred Kochen, and Eugene Garfield are enthusiastic proponents of the international coordination and dissemination of the world's knowledge to solve the problems of mankind. Inspired by the writings of H. G. Wells, they call their hoped-for product "The World Brain" or "The World Encyclopedia."[12]

THE EQUAL DISTRIBUTION OF INFORMATION

A strong faith in the benevolent result of the integration and internationalization of knowledge leads to a third major idea of those who are influential in Western international and comparative librarianship: the concept that information generated in the West—particularly information of economic value—should be made available throughout the world. E. J. Josey sums this up with his statement: "Equal distribution of data is certainly needed on the international level."[13] Like Josey, Joseph Z. Nitecki extrapolates from a concept sometimes applied at a national level and declares that the failure of libraries to cooperate internationally to give full information access to *all* is "discriminatory."[14] However, the free flow of information is frequently opposed when there is a perception that it may in some way promote Western influence in the world. Thus, while the governments of the United States and Great Britain have consistently fought the efforts of the communist countries and the Third World to bring about a "New World Information and Communication Order," it is supported by many of those active in the field of international librarianship.[15]

A fourth concept generally accepted by those active in this field is the belief that centralized planning and government direction and assistance will be needed to attain the goals of international librarianship. (Interestingly, this coexists with the apparently contradictory belief that governments have failed to bring the people of the world together.) Kryzs and Litton predict that during the lifetime of their readers "Within each country certainly, or within a world government possibly, legislation will be enacted that will assure the realization of the constituent elements of a global librarianship."[16]

Vosper strongly supports central planning and government involvement, noting that the USSR has been the world's leader in this with the West trailing, but improving.[17] Foskett implies that the centralization found in Eastern Europe never actually stemmed from communist political philosophy but rather from a desire for efficiency.[18] In an article on the international library education, Martha Boaz attributes the failure to centralize American international education to the fact that the United States does not have a ministry of education.[19] She quotes from *World Education; An Emerging Concept*: 'It will only be a matter of time until one world government is formed, unless separate national loyalties through gross miscalculation and chauvinistic aims destroy us first.'[20] Frederick Kilgour expresses the less commonly heard view that it is the United States, rather than the highly centralized countries, which is promoting the free international exchange of information.[21]

CULTURAL RELATIVISM

A major reason why many Western leaders in this field have been optimistic about the possibilities of international cooperation is that they have seen strong underlying similarities among apparently disparate social and political systems, e.g., between democratic and communist societies. Thus in the 1960's, Foskett remarked that in Eastern Europe the library was expected, among other things, to foster communist propaganda. Some in the West would disagree, he noted,

> ... but it is no different, in principle, from the patriotic fervour displayed by some American libraries in praising the American way of life. In fact it would be hard to find a really vital public library that was not, in one way or another, committed to the attainment of objectives that its society held to be worthwhile. We in this country [The United Kingdom], for example, cheerfully involve our public libraries in such things as productivity campaigns; do we ever pause to ask ourselves what is the aim of such campaigns?[22]

Similarly, in 1973 Harvey wrote:

> In a socialist country with a strong, central government, like Bulgaria, certain differences of organization and administration can be expected when comparison is made with Switzerland, having a different political and economic system. However, this paper assumes most of these to be differences in practice, not in policies, principles or goals. Perhaps, even USSR libraries can be examined by an American with standards modified only partially.
> The degree to which libraries in Bulgaria and Switzerland are comparable would decrease primarily as their goals differed. Of course, school library service philosophy, in socialist countries, for instance, is tied closely to the political, economic and social systems and attempts to reinforce them with many books explaining the socialist philosophy. However, political books in capitalist country school libraries are likely to explain the local political system, also.[23]

H. Allen Whatley finds many similarities between the philosophy of book distribution in communist countries and that in the West, and equates Stalin's purges of library bookshelves in the 1920's and 1930's with the practice found in democratic countries of relegating some volumes to restricted-access collections.[24]

The playing down of distinctions among different societies is facilitated by the discouragement of value judgements, which are considered to be relative, and therefore moot.[25] It has even been stated that the successful international library worker is distinguished by a "lack of strong political and ethical ideas, his blandness. In fact, he finds strong feelings of any kind likely to be inhibiting and obsolete."[26] To some extent, this approach is engendered by a desire to create a science of comparative librarianship. However, another influential factor is indicated by a criticism expressed by one of those involved in the field, A. D. Burnett: the tendency for Westerners to omit the full truth from their reports on other countries because of their desire to promote international harmony.[27]

Interestingly, it has been considered productive in this field to praise the countries of Eastern Europe and the developing world while criticizing the West. As already noted, some of these judgements revolve around the centralization of library affairs and the international dissemination of information. At one conference on international librarianship, Patricia Schuman and E. J. Josey devoted much of their speeches to criticizing the United States.[28]

According to veterans in this area of the profession, even the Western librarian who attempts to assist other countries is suspect:

1. The International Man must be ever on guard against neocolonialism. His ideal is service, but his obligation is also to counteract Western money and guns. Is he subtly peddling political or religious views along with his suggestions and advice?[29]
2. We do not think of ourselves in political terms when we offer professional assistance to libraries, but the political implications are always in the minds of our hosts. Our protestation that we have no motivation other than pure altruism and professional commitment must contend with the incontrovertible fact that history, both ours and theirs, argues against so innocent an intentions.[30]

It is held that library school courses in international and comparative librarianship should impart to students the basic philosophy described in this article. (In addition, the idea that all courses in library and information science must be taught from an international perspective is gaining popularity.[31]) J. Periam Danton, Martha Boaz, and Sylva Simsova state that courses on the international and comparative aspects of library and information science should advance international cooperation and understanding.[32] Frances Carroll concludes an article on the subject with the view that "the many [international] library education activists should continue, and they will be nurtured by the forces of an international society."[33]

CONCLUSION

In sum, the Anglo-American leaders of international and comparative library and information science generally agree that we live in a Global Village and must work for a unified profession in a unified world. They maintain that information must be "integrated" to form a World Brain, which should then be used to solve the earth's problems. Such activities—in which librarians would be key—require an increased centralization of power, particularly at the international level. This restructuring, we are told, would curtail Western hegemony in the area of information and ensure global understanding, peace, and justice. The creation of such a scientific, internationalist profession apparently also necessitates self-criticism on the part of Western nations, and the avoidance of value judgements when dealing with communist or developing countries.

Given the durability of these beliefs in Western librarianship—particularly in the United States and Great Britain—it is not improbable that they will continue unchanged, barring some cataclysmic event.

REFERENCES

1. John F. Harvey, "Toward A Definition of International and Comparative Library Science," *International Library Review* 5 (July 1973): 294. It should be noted that he claims to reject the social/idealistic aspects of the philosophy as inappropriate and impractical. He wants comparative librarianship to become a field of scholarship, justifiable in and of itself.

2. Lester Asheim, *Librarianship in the Developing Countries* (Urbana: University of Illinois Press, 1966), p. 2.

3. B.C. Vickery and A.G. Brown, "Information Science," *Comparative*

and International Library Science, ed. by John F. Harvey (Metuchen, NJ, and London: Scarecrow Press, 1977), p. 190.

4. Allen Kent and Harold Lancour, "Preface," *Encyclopedia of Library and Information Science*, vol. 1, ed. by Kent and Lancour (New York: Marcel Dekker, 1968), p. xii.

5. Sylva Simsova, "Comparative Librarianship as an Academic Subject," *Journal of Librarianship* 6 (April 1974): 116.

6. Ibid., p. 117.

7. In *World Librarianship: A Comparative Study*, by Richard Krzys and Gaston Litton, with Ann Hewitt (New York and Basel: Marcel Dekker, 1983), pp. 201-3.

8. D.J. Foskett, "Comparative Librarianship," *Progress in Library Science*, ed. by Robert L. Collison (London: Butterworths, 1965), p. 144.

9. Louis Shores, "Comparative Librarianship: A Theoretical Approach," *Comparative and International Librarianship*, ed. by Miles M. Jackson (Westport, CT: Greenwood Press, 1970), p. 4. See also p. 23. Unlike many involved in international librarianship, Shores holds a positive view of America and other Western countries.

10. Robert Vosper, "National and International Library Planning," *National and International Library Planning* (Munich: Verlag Dokumentation, 1976), pp. 11-14.

11. Ibid., p. 11.

12. H.J. Abraham Goodman, "The 'World Brain/World Encyclopedia' Concept," *ASIS '87: Proceedings of the 50th Annual Conference of the ASIS [American Society for Information Science] Annual Meeting* (Medford, NJ: Learned Information, 1987), pp. 91-98, 256.

13. E.J. Josey, "Political Dimensions of International Librarianship," speech, New York City, Library Association of the City University of New York Institute: *Shrinking World, Exploding Information: Developments in International Librarianship*, April 4, 1986. A videotape of The Institute's proceedings is available from the Library Association of C.U.N.Y.

14. Joseph Z. Nitecki, "National Network of Information in Poland," *Journal of the American Society for Information Science* 30 (Sept. 1979): 274-79.

15. See, for example: Thomas T. Surprenant, "Global Threats to Information," *Annual Review of Information Science and Technology* vol. 20 (White Plains, NY: Knowledge Industry Publications, 1985) and R.C. Benge, *Confessions of a Lapsed Librarian* (Metuchen, NJ: Scarecrow Press, 1984), pp. 185-205. Bro. Emmett Corry has referred to "the phobic attempts of this country [The United States] to control the Third World's access to both technological information and communications channels." In *Unequal Access to Information Resources: Problems and Needs of the World's Information Poor* (Ann Arbor, MI: Pierian Press, 1988), p. v.

16. *World Librarianship*, p. 201.

17. Vosper, p. 10 and elsewhere.

18. Foskett, p. 132.

19. Martha Boaz, "International Education: An Imperative Need," *Journal of Education for Library and Information Science* 26 (Winter 1986): 172.
20. M.R. Mitchell, S.S. Grin, and B. Sobel (Washington, DC: University Press of America, 1977), p. 65, note 3; as cited by Boaz, p. 173.
21. Frederick Kilgour, "Public Policy and National and International Networks," *Libraries and Information Science in the Electronic Age* (Philadelphia, PA: ISI Press, 1986), pp. 1-10.
22. Foskett, pp. 136-37.
23. Harvey, "Toward a Definition of International and Comparative Library Science," p. 314.
24. H. Allen Whatley, "European Librarianship," *The Library in Society*, by A. Robert Rogers, Kathryn McChesney, and others (Littleton, CO: LIbraries Unlimited, 1984), p. 132.
25. See, for example, Simsova, pp. 117-20.
26. John Harvey, "An Anatomy of the International Man," *Wilson Library Bulletin*, 47 (June 1973): 841.
27. A.D. Burnett, "Study in Comparative Librarianship, I," *Studies in Comparative Librarianship* (London: The Library Association, 1973), pp. 7-8.
28. Patricia Schuman, "Recent Developments in U.S. Information Policy"; and E.J. Josey, "Political Dimensions of International Librarianship," *Shrinking World, Exploding Information*.
29. Harvey, "Anatomy," p. 841.
30. Asheim, p. 67.
31. A rationale and detailed plan for internationalizing the curriculum is presented in *Internationalizing Library and Information Science Education: A Handbook of Policies and Procedures in Administration and Curriculum*, ed. by John F. Harvey and Frances Laverne Carroll (New York and London: Greenwood Press, 1987).
32. J. Periam Danton, *The Dimensions of Comparative Librarianship* (Chicago: American Library Association, 1973); Martha Boaz, "The Comparative and International Library Science Course in American Library Schools," *Comparative and International Library Science*, pp. 169-74; and Simsova, p. 121.
33. Frances Laverne Carroll, "Library Education," *Comparative and International Library Science*, pp. 160-61.

Strengthening the Foundation for Information Literacy in an Academic Library

Laura A. Sullivan
Nancy F. Campbell

SUMMARY. The relationship between the library and the information literacy movement is acknowledged, and a further delineation of responsibility at the academic reference service level is examined. Reference librarians' perspective enables them to serve as "information advisors," fostering students' development of information literacy skills. As technology continues to drive information storage and retrieval, this role becomes increasingly important. The need for students to emerge as independent learners is crucial at this stage in their lives. Information literacy abilities are discussed as a by-product of general reference functions. Reference librarians are urged to encourage the growth of these abilities by stimulating students' understanding of critical thinking.

In an extensive and cogent report released in January 1989, the American Library Association's Presidential Committee on Information Literacy asked libraries to take a proactive role in the information literacy challenge. The report defines information literate people as "those who have learned how to learn . . . because they know how knowledge is organized, how to find information, and how to use information in such a way that others can learn from them. They are people prepared for lifelong learning . . . " (1).

The topic of information literacy and the library's relationship with it has been steadily gaining momentum. In the literature, Kuhlthau (1987) defined information literacy as a combination of library skills and computer literacy; Breivik (1987) and Gee and Breivik

---

Laura A. Sullivan is Head of Public Services and Nancy F. Campbell is Head of Reference at Steely Library, Northern Kentucky University, Highland Heights, KY 41076.

(1987) discuss the library as a crucial factor in undergraduate education and call for universities to rethink their view of the library's/librarian's role on campus. Symposiums and conferences on information literacy have taken place; also, Patricia Berger, ALA President 1989-90, states as one of her main concerns "the growing problem of illiteracy and the librarian's role in solving it" (Letter 1989).

While information literacy and the librarian's part in it may be an idea new to some educators, administrators and business people, the librarian has known for years the role she/he plays in this area. Tuckett and Stoffle (1984) identified a "self-reliant library user" as a "successful bibliographic problem-solver who learns through information use" (58). Self-reliant skills obtained through library use will enable individuals to "deal with the basic requirements of our information-based democratic society . . . " and they "will also be able to function more effectively as independent learners, continuing to grow intellectually outside the structure and requirements of formal education" (59). These ideas have surfaced in the current information literacy literature. Even Tuckett and Stoffle acknowledge Otis Robinson's 1876 belief that a librarian is an educator and responsible for the self-reliance of students.

It is hoped that those concerned with the information literacy issue will understand and "buy into" the library's importance in molding information literates. This article acknowledges the reference librarian as a key contributor to the information literacy crusade.

One of the most positive aspects of reference librarianship is the ability to influence individuals to become independent learners. At the symposium on "Libraries and the Search for Academic Excellence" (Breivik 1987), Ernest Boyer stated

> Those in charge of information services on a campus are the renaissance people who are able to guide students through the typology of knowledge and help them discover the relationships that no single department and no single professor can provide (46).

Academic reference librarians are the "renaissance people" and their contribution to information literacy can be viewed as a result of two factors: (1) the nature of reference work in a university library and (2) the general level of maturity attained by its students.

College students and community patrons who regularly use an academic library can be greatly impacted by the reference services offered. A certain dichotomy exists in reference work in all types of libraries—one side presents the issue of providing information to users while the other side advocates facilitating users to effectively use information sources themselves.

By definition reference service in an academic library endorses the philosophy of teaching/enabling users to become self-sufficient in the library. Reports of unobtrusive studies to measure reference accuracy are not substantially relevant when evaluating reference service with a teaching philosophy. College and university reference librarians are more likely to measure their contribution to students' success in developing search strategies and gaining proficiency in using information sources effectively. Certainly there are instances when providing an answer is necessary and accuracy in doing so is essential. However, within the context of an educational institution, the mission of the college or university is extended to the library through the knowledge attained by students learning to use the library and its resources. One of the recommendations of the 1989 ALA Information Literacy report states that a teacher should serve as "a facilitator of student learning rather than as presenter of ready-made information" (13). This statement emphatically applies to reference librarians as well.

Reference librarians hold a unique vantage point regarding information literacy by experiencing first-hand the needs and capabilities of users. Reference librarians in particular can contribute to the development of information literacy abilities. An astute reference librarian will be a composite of the necessary information-seeking skills and knowledge of sources; therefore, the stage is set to actively engage in transforming passive users into active ones.

THE REFERENCE ENVIRONMENT

The opportunities for moving users toward an independent learning style occur primarily in three situations: one-to-one at the reference desk, within the reference environs and during the library instruction session.

Although trying to impress critical thinking skills upon a student at the reference desk may be tenuous at best, the reference interchange is a good starting point. Numerous situations arise which encourage application of information literacy aptitudes:

- Stressing selectivity when choosing citations in an index and identifying "clues" that can determine quality of an article.
- Suggesting a subject encyclopedia when beginning research to gain understanding of a topic or to refine a topic.
- Pointing out overlooked pieces of information on a catalog record: date of publication, bibliography included, etc.
- Explaining the difference between a scholarly journal and a popular magazine when suggesting indexes for a topic.

If a student chooses not to seek the services of the reference librarian, subliminal means are available which can direct the user. For example, the reference department can be organized with the student in mind by grouping like subject tools together. This encourages a self-directed approach to research. Other means of subliminal assistance include ample signage and adequate point-of-use instructional aids.

To take this idea one step further, the online public access catalog can be an instrument in teaching critical thinking. The online catalog at Dickinson College, AutoCat, was designed with exactly this goal in mind. The AutoCat team realized that "if AutoCat were to become an important educational tool, it would need to enhance the critical use of information rather than the mere finding of it" (Bechtel 1988, 31). As a result of the system's protocols, users are required to demonstrate skills attributed to the information literate; these include evaluating information, recognizing various viewpoints and questioning "facts." Bechtel also makes the point that learning to use the online catalog by these methods is more interesting and stimulating to the student than merely mastering its mechanics (39).

The third opportunity for presenting an evaluative approach to research is in a library instruction session. Ideas only touched on during a reference interchange are presented in more depth in the classroom. Here is where information literacy skills are encouraged, explained and demonstrated — through examples prepared by the reference librarian and through subsequent discussion/group work among the students. Assignments or exercises distinctly designed to arouse students' consciousness regarding bias, accuracy, etc. in a newspaper article, for example, can be most effective.

Again, the time limitation exists. But most importantly, students are exposed to the concept of a research strategy and are asked to think *beyond* their immediate assignment. They are asked to begin acquiring skills—" . . . how to find, analyze, synthesize, evaluate, and communicate information and ideas" (Pelzman 1989, 82)— that will carry them from one tool to the next, one assignment to the next and from one life situation to another. Moreover, as Breivik and Gee (1987) point out " . . . students need to understand . . . If they finish their education thinking that libraries are only useful for classroom assignments and recreational reading they are not information literate. Indeed, it is this transferability that is the essence of information literacy" (19-20).

THE TECHNOLOGICAL TRANSITION

Technology continues to drive how information is organized, stored and accessed. As "renaissance people" reference librarians must direct their efforts even more towards self-sufficiency in light of these developments. As the trend continues towards more nonprint information storage and retrieval, it is largely a responsibility of the reference librarian to serve as an "advisor" or guide through the myriad amount of information.

A typical university library may offer a variety of automated resources, such as CD-ROM services, an online catalog and end-user searching of databases. A popular misconception among library users is that information stored in a computerized format is the ultimate, "what-else-could-I-possibly-need" source. A major task for reference librarians is to dispel this myth and help users discern among the wide range of tools. It is vitally important to overcome users' infatuation with technology and help them realize that, no matter the format, their skill at accessing, evaluating and synthesizing information is the key to effective research.

Reference professionals, in tandem with educators, need to cultivate the concept of lifelong learning through information literacy skills, developed both in the classroom and in the library. With the "information explosion" continuing to resound, the effect reference librarians can make on individual "questioning" behavior is significant. Reference librarians must encourage students to question their findings every step of the way in the research process, especially as new formats are made available. Information literacy is not the "how" of information-gathering, but rather the "why" — understanding and evaluating what is found.

THE AGE FACTOR

A primary reason that reference librarians are able to augment the information literateness of students is that the student and librarian meet "in the right place at the right time." At the college or university level, the concepts behind "learning how to learn" begin to solidify and lifelong applications are, perhaps for the first time, put into proper perspective. Understandably, it is important to introduce these concepts at an early age; however, their significance is not fully realized until the individual is confronted with more sophisticated needs.

At this stage of life, the traditional college student is designing a career path and with the help of academic advisors, is planning the curriculum to pave the way. The reference librarian can have an "advisory" function as well as an instructional one, concomitant to that of the teaching faculty. By realizing that these students are faced now with an overwhelming number of choices in everyday situations, the librarian can increase their chances to function capably and independently in the next phase of their lives.

Ernest Boyer (Breivik 1987) further elaborates on the "connectivity" role between libraries and students in the pursuit of academic excellence:

> ... as students go along toward more and more maturity, they should become increasingly self-sufficient and independent as learners. Instead of depending upon signals from the professor, they should be able to move into the library and its resources and become self-directed. (46)

It is at this convergence that the reference librarian moves to the forefront and assumes guidance of the student.

CONCLUSION

The academic reference librarian as described here exists in the ideal sense—where he/she internalizes and personifies the information literate's characteristics and then promotes these behaviors in daily work/life. Not all reference librarians are in accordance with the philosophy which fosters an independent style of learning. However, as information literacy becomes a greater concern nationally and as the library becomes a focal point in amending the situation, reference librarians have the responsibility to champion the progress.

REFERENCES

1. American Library Association. Presidential Committee on Information Literacy. Final Report. January 1989.
2. Bechtel, J. 1988. Developing and using the online catalog to teach critical thinking. *Information Technology and Libraries* 7(March):30-40.
3. Berger, P.W. 1989. Letter to American Library Association Membership.
4. Breivik, P.S. 1987. Making the most of libraries. *Change* 19(July/August):44-52.
5. Gee, E.G., and P.S. Breivik. 1987. *Libraries and learning*. Paper presented as part of the symposium "Libraries and the search for academic excellence" at New York, NY, 15-17 March. ERIC, ED 284 593.
6. Kuhlthau, C.C. (1987. *Information skills for an information society: A review of research. An ERIC Information Analysis Product*. Washington, DC: Office of Educational Research and Improvement. ERIC, ED 297 740.
7. Pelzman, F. 1989. Information literacy—a common ground. *Wilson Library Bulletin* 63(June):82-83.
8. Tuckett, H.W., & C.J. Stoffle. 1984. Learning theory and the self-reliant library user. *RQ* 24(Fall):58-66.

Community Cooperation in Reference Service via a Librarians' Liaison Committee

Margaret Hendley

SUMMARY. Busy reference desks in academic libraries have more than enough to do to try to meet the information and reference needs of the students, faculty and staff in their own institutions. Any college or university library, however, that is located in an urban or suburban environment will undoubtably face a demand for service from high school students and their teachers, particularly in locations where increased emphasis is placed on research and independent study in the secondary school curriculum. The University of Waterloo Library responded to this need by working cooperatively with secondary school libraries and public libraries in the community through the creation of a Librarians' Liaison Committee. The on-going work of this committee has resulted in the delivery of a highly successful service to this segment of the local population.

The concept of information literacy is one advocated by reference librarians from a variety of types of institutions. Since the early '80's it has been the topic of numerous papers and the theme of many conferences, culminating in 1989 in the publication of the book, *Information Literacy*, written by Patricia Breivik, who could be called the guru in this field.[1]

In an earlier publication, Breivik outlines some of the main features of this concept: (1) the recognition of the need to prepare students for life-long learning; (2) the need for students to be able to construct information search strategies to locate, evaluate and effectively use information; and (3) removal of the reliance by students,

---

Margaret Hendley is Coordinator, User Education, University Library, University of Waterloo, Waterloo, Ontario. N2L 3G1.

© 1991 by The Haworth Press, Inc. All rights reserved.

(or any user), on the resources belonging ONLY to their particular institution.[2]

It is the consequences of carrying out this philosophy of information literacy in a particular community by a particular group of learners that is the focus of this paper, specifically secondary school students using the academic libraries and to some extent, the other libraries, in the Regional Municipality of Waterloo, Ontario for course-related research purposes. (The population of this region is approximately 354,000. It has a total of twenty secondary schools run by either the Waterloo County Board of Education, or the Separate School Board and three private secondary schools. There are two universities in the area, University of Waterloo and Wilfrid Laurier University. Each municipality within the Region is served by a public library. In addition, there are a number of special libraries with varying policies regarding public use.)

It is obvious then that a student in this Region seeking resources for research outside of the perimeters of his/her school library would be faced with a wide variety of choices. However, in a less than ideal world where the effectiveness of a given institution is judged almost solely on the service given to its particular user group, and funding for that institution is based most definitely on the primary community that it serves, it can be difficult to allocate the staff time and library resources to serve the needs of a group viewed as outside the primary user group.

Although independent research has long been a component of many high school courses, it is only in recent years that it has received such an emphasis. In Ontario the ground work was laid by the Ontario Ministry of Education with its 1982 publication of *Partners in Action: the Library Resource Centre in the School Curriculum*. While this document concentrates on the role of the Library Resource Centre and the teacher-librarian taking a central role in the students' use of non-textbook resources for learning, it also discusses the place of other libraries in the community such as academic or public libraries for research purposes. It points out the role of the teacher-librarian as a consultant to the classroom teachers when determining just where in the community the best resources for a particular research topic can be located.[3] This consultant role became vital to the guidelines which were established in the Region to provide effective multi-agency cooperation to meet the research needs of secondary school students.

This change to an emphasis on independent studies in the local schools was documented more recently by a 1989 report which summarized the Independent Research Requirements for each subject taught in the Region based on Ontario Ministry of Education Guidelines. This publication was written by a local teacher-librarian, Dr. Robert Derksen, and the Librarian's Curriculum Committee.[4] The result of this emphasis had been felt locally with large numbers of students requesting help in using academic library resources as well as requests from local teachers for bibliographic instruction in the academic libraries for classes of high school students.

IMPACT ON ACADEMIC LIBRARIES

The already busy reference desks in the two academic libraries had more than enough to do to try and meet the information and reference needs of the students, faculty and staff in their own institutions. And of course, the librarians responsible for user education in these university libraries felt overwhelmed at the thought of adding a whole new user group to their responsibilities without any established guidelines or control over the requests from the secondary schools. However much these academic librarians would agree philosophically with the concept of information literacy and its implications of freedom from being bound to any one source of information or institution, the realities of dealing with it face to face was viewed with dismay. What could have resulted in a very understandably self-protective insular reaction to this situation, however, provided instead the incentive for a cooperative approach by representative librarians from the institutions involved to try and work out a solution.

An initial meeting in the fall of 1987 was held with librarians from the two universities in the Region, the University of Waterloo and Wilfrid Laurier University, with representative teacher-librarians from the Waterloo County Board of Education.[5] A discussion of some of the specific problems of secondary school students visiting the academic libraries individually or in classes was set forth. The problems with the current situation from the point of view of the academic librarians were outlined as:

1. use of staff time which was at a premium due to general financial restraints
2. offering group or individual user education instruction to local high school students may deflect attention from the primary academic community
3. requests for class visits and bibliographic instruction usually came directly from the individual teachers with no contact with the teacher-librarian in a particular school
4. resources which were borrowed from the academic library may disadvantage the primary users and may cause problems with retrieval

Those representing the local secondary schools were particularly concerned that the teachers requesting class visits usually acted independently without prior consultation with their teacher-librarian. They felt that the teachers should first discuss the course related information needs of their students with the teacher-librarian so that the best place to do the necessary research can be determined. If it is decided that an academic or other local library is the best place for the students' independent research, the teacher-librarian can then make the appropriate arrangements and see that the students be properly prepared in terms of their level of research skills, for using the resources of another library.

The result of this, and other meetings, was the creation of a manual for secondary school students, teachers and teacher-librarians wishing to use the academic libraries of the University of Waterloo and Wilfrid Laurier University. This manual combined two functions: (1) it provided relevant information about the two university libraries; (2) it established guidelines to be followed when secondary school students and/or their teachers wished to use the resources and services, including bibliographic instruction, of the academic libraries. Copies of the manual were distributed to the local high schools and the two university libraries.

Librarians' Liaison Committee

The following year, when the group, now termed the Librarians' Liaison Committee, met to discuss the effectiveness of their guidelines and how to revise and update the manual, a representative from the Kitchener Public Library was included. KPL was the largest public library in the Region with an active user education program for its public. This library also had experienced the effects of dealing with large numbers of secondary students doing course-related independent research as well as teachers requesting class visits with special user education workshops or presentations for their students. The concerns of the public librarians in trying to effectively meet the information needs of this particular user group had many similarities with issues raised by their academic colleagues. Of particular interest was the lack of coordination with the local teacher-librarians, so that each request for a class visit was independent and lacking any collaborative effort with the teacher-librarian who might help prepare the students for such visits. When the new edition of the manual was published that year by the Librarians' Liaison Committee it included a section on how secondary schools could request class visits and user education workshops at the Kitchener Public Library. The following year the Waterloo Public Library and a local special library, belonging to the Global Community Centre, joined the committee and were included in the manual.

A central feature of the whole process was the consultative role of the secondary school teacher-librarian within their own school. (See Appendix A: The Roles of the Secondary Teacher-Librarian and Community Librarians in the Liaison Process.) Equally important to the cooperative and problem-solving approach taken by the organizations represented on the committee was the fact that each had a designated librarian who would act as the contact for that library and the liaison with the secondary school teacher-librarian. Thus any particular instances, such as a group of high school students showing up unannounced at the Information Desk of one of the academic libraries and stating that their teacher had sent them to do research at that library even though they had no idea how to proceed, could be dealt with effectively in a cooperative problem-solving approach by those most familiar with the established guidelines. Even more importantly, teacher-librarians would work with the teachers in their schools to recommend the most appropriate resources, in or out of the secondary school system, for the students to use for their research needs; when community resources were deemed appropriate, they would discuss these specific research needs with the contact at the local academic, public, or special library and would prepare the secondary school students for any upcoming class visits to these libraries.

The academic libraries fine-tuned this preparation with a Skills Chart Checklist for all secondary school students using university libraries which was published in the manual. This checklist included such areas as general library orientation, organization of resources, and selection and utilization of resources. (See Appendix B. Skills Chart Checklist.) It was particularly useful that efforts were made so that high school students would enter the university library at least aware that its resources were organized according to the Library of Congress Classification scheme, and would know at least the basics of using periodical indexes. It should be noted that in addition, the University of Waterloo Library required that any high school student wishing to apply for a library borrowers' card had to have a special application form signed by their school's teacher-librarian who confirmed that the student possessed the library skills listed in the Skills Chart Checklist. (See Appendix C. UW Library High School Borrowers' Application Form.) Also, the two university libraries limited their service of offering bibliographic instruction to high school classes to those who were taking courses designated as Ontario Academic Credit courses. (These were various final year courses which were requirements for university acceptance.)

The public and special libraries, in keeping with their mandate to serve the general public, did not require any skills checklist to be completed, nor did they restrict their presentations and/or research workshops to only the upper classmen in the high schools. They did, however, require the liaison with the teacher-librarians and their cooperation in preparing students for any requested class visits. All of the participating libraries also set guidelines regarding such specifics as the amount of notice necessary prior to "booking" a class visit and any restrictions regarding the time of year that workshops would be offered to outside groups.

How effective have these guidelines been? It is fair to state that all of the libraries involved have felt that they have benefited from participation in the group. The teacher-librarians have seen their consultative and liaison functions properly utilized; the academic, public and special librarians now have a coordinated approach which introduces a measure of control into their efforts to work with this particular user group; and, perhaps, most importantly, the students themselves can begin to use effectively a variety of library resources in their community. By these efforts some major steps have been taken to provide the beginnings of information literacy for at least one user group in the area.

Communication between the librarians in these different institutions has improved and insight gained into the realities of librarianship in other institutions. Situations involving particular schools or groups of students can be dealt with by a problem-solving approach between the relevant teacher-librarian and the contact librarian. Additional ways were sought to improve the understanding between the groups involved which included visits by the contact librarians to one of the regular meetings of the teacher-librarians in the community. Also, both the Kitchener Public Library and the University of Waterloo Library have given special research workshops to the teachers and the teacher-librarians for one of their Professional Development Days.

Future Goals

The future goals of the Librarians' Liaison committee include broadening the representation of the committee to include other public and special libraries in the Region, as well as introducing representation by the local Community College. A more comprehensive networking capability could be introduced as more of the participating libraries automate their systems.

It is not the particular objectives and guidelines of the Librarians' Liaison Committee that is important here. Other university libraries faced with similar situations have sought other creative ways of dealing with the problem of how to handle local students who wish to learn how to use an academic library.[6] Also, although the objective of this committee was related clearly to the research needs of local secondary school students, they are not the only group who would benefit from such an approach. For example, in some areas, university students who take academic courses through distance education do not have an academic or large public library in the area. Clearly, providing library support to their university's distance education students is an active concern of academic librarians as evidenced in the Checklist of Common Practices published as part of a conference proceedings focused on academic off-campus library services.[7] In addition, however, it is possible to consider that a percentage of these distance education students who live in isolated rural communities would benefit also from first hand research experience if allowed access to the resources of the local secondary school library if that is the largest research resource in the vicinity.

The concept of information literacy is ill served if libraries interpret too rigidly the perimeters of their particular user group. The need for cooperation among different types of libraries to meet the information and research needs of various user groups has become more acute in light of today's escalating costs. Ironically, with increasingly sophisticated means of automation, access to resources thousands of miles away is sometimes easier to achieve than a sharing among libraries in a given community.

REFERENCES

1. Breivik, Patricia. *Information Literacy: Revolution in the Library*. (New York: American Council on Education, 1989).

2. Breivik, Patricia. "Library Based Learning in an Information Society," *New Directions for Higher Education*, Winter 1986, pp. 48-49.

3. Ontario. Ministry of Education. *Partners in Action: The Library Resource Centre in the School Curriculum*. (Toronto, 1982.)

4. *Independent Research Requirements Involving the Secondary School Library Resource Centre*. (Report of the Curriculum Committee, R.C. Derkson, Chairman. Waterloo County Board of Education, June 1989.)

5. I wish to thank Dr. Gary Draper, Librarian at St. Jerome's College, University of Waterloo and Dr. Robert Derksen, Head of the Library at Waterloo Collegiate, for their generous contribution to this paper. Also to Linda Leger, who as

previous Coordinator, User Education at the University of Waterloo, played a significant role in the beginning years of the Liaison Committee.

6. Hammond, Carol. "Aliens in the House: Those Other Students Who Use Your Library," *Research Strategies*, Summer 1989. pp. 134-137.

7. *The Off-Campus Library Services Conference Proceedings. Knoxville, Tennessee, April 18-19, 1985*. ed. by Barton M. Lessin. (Mount Pleasant, Michigan: Central Michigan Press, 1986) p. 183.

8. Appendices taken from the manual *A Guide for Secondary School Students, Teachers and Teacher-Librarians to Library Resources in the Kitchener-Waterloo Area, 1989-1990*. written by Librarians Liaison Committee.

APPENDIX A

The Roles of the Secondary Teacher-Librarian and Community Librarians in the Liaison Process

Part of the mandate which the Ontario Ministry of Education expects teacher-librarians to fulfill is developing "... working relationships with other school libraries, community organizations, and external resources." (Partners in Action, 1982, p. 14)

Given the communications process laid out in this document, librarians at the two university libraries and the three public library systems, as well as community organizations such as Global, can expect the following:

1. Teacher-librarians make their school administration, teachers and students aware of the liaison policies in effect.

2. Teacher-librarians are willing to provide individual users with the information and skills needed to use other libraries.

3. Teacher-librarians authorize OAC students to obtain university library cards upon being satisfied that the students are sufficiently knowledgeable and responsible.

4. Teacher-librarians work co-operatively with teachers and other libraries' librarians to prepare students for class visits.

5. Teacher-librarians respond to information from the other libraries' librarians concerning any problems encountered by the school's staff and students.

To allow teacher-librarians to complete these tasks successfully, the community librarians at the two universities, three public library systems and community organizations such as Global, must undertake to do the following:

1. Librarians provide all reasonable help to secondary school students.
2. Librarians take down pertinent information on student use (eg. school, course, teacher, assignment) if individual students seem to be faltering in the research process.
3. Librarians follow up on Item #2 by making immediate contact with the school's Head of Library.
4. Librarians only allow class bookings through the school's Head of Library.
5. Librarians are willing to join a consultative process with teachers through the school's teacher-librarians.

Taken from the guide prepared by the Librarians' Liaison Committee 1990-1991.

APPENDIX B

Skills Chart Checklist

For all Secondary Students Using University Libraries

A. Library Orientation - Students know how to:

___ 1. locate the university library
___ 2. observe the university library's rules for behaviour
___ 3. find appropriate work areas in the university library
___ 4. obtain a library card when appropriate (and know the rules!)
___ 5. identify various kinds of material available in the library
___ 6. handle material properly
___ 7. locate the relevant sources
___ 8. locate information flyers and pamphlets at the university library

B. Organization of Resources - Students are familiar with the following categories of resources:

___ 1. fiction and non-fiction books
___ 2. general reference materials
___ 3. audio-visual materials
___ 4. periodicals
___ 5. vertical-file material
___ 6. periodical indexes
___ 7. the Library of Congress classification scheme
___ 8. serials list on microfiche

C. *Selection of Resources - Students are able to:*

___ 1. *use the online catalogue to perform author, title and subject searches*
___ 2. *locate materials according to call number*
___ 3. *use the catalogue as a selection tool*
___ 4. *proceed from general to specific or specific to general when researching a topic*
___ 5. *select general and specialized reference materials*
___ 6. *evaluate material for currency*
___ 7. *use a bibliography to select additional information*

D: *Utilization of Resources - Students know:*

___ 1. *the parts and aspects of a book*
___ 2. *how to use periodical indexes*
___ 3. *how to distinguish among primary, secondary and tertiary sources*
___ 4. *how to select materials appropriate to their level*
___ 5. *how to interpret and write footnotes*
___ 6. *the facilities such as study areas and photocopy arrangements*
___ 7. *discretion in using resource personnel meant for the university community*

Taken from the guide prepared by the Librarians' Liaison Committee 1990-1991.

APPENDIX C

HIGH SCHOOL BORROWER APPLICATION FORM

NAME: _____

SCHOOL: _____

GRADE OR YEAR: _____

RECOMMENDATION OF THE TEACHER-LIBRARIAN OR PRINCIPAL

The above-named student requests the privilege of becoming a borrower at the University of Waterloo Library during the current academic year. I am satisfied that this student's course work necessitates the borrowing of materials held in the UW Library which are not available in the high school or public library, including, for example (e.g. topic or title):

_____

This student is a knowledgeable and responsible library user at this school and, in my judgment, understands and will abide by the requirements of the UW Library. In addition, this student possesses the library skills listed in the Skills Chart Checklist provided overleaf.

Signed: _____   Position/Title: _____

Date: _____   Expiration Date: _____
                                (expires no later than April 30 of
                                current academic year)

STUDENT DECLARATION

I understand that in accepting the privilege of becoming a borrower at the University of Waterloo Library, I accept as well the responsibility of following all the guidelines and regulations laid down for all UW Library users. I understand that these regulations include the requirement that borrowed materials be returned on or before their due date, the levy of late return fees for overdue items, and the payment of replacement costs for lost items.

Signed: _____   Date: _____

Volunteers and Reference Services with a Special Collection

Anne F. Roberts

SUMMARY. With budget cuts facing most academic institutions, many collections go unprocessed and unused without adequate professional staff to process or service them. One group of manuscripts that was of interest to the library had potential interest to a particular group of people in the community. Targeted individuals in the community were solicited to assist as volunteers in processing the collection. This was a successful and creative way to help in a time of financial straits.

The experience of the library at the State University of New York (Albany) illustrates one use of volunteers and suggests how they may be used in other settings for other assignments. Public libraries have traditionally used volunteers. Academic libraries have been less active in using volunteers because of the staff time and other variables that are involved in recruiting, training, and maintaining volunteers.

Falling budgets as well as other fiscal constraints have forced librarians to come up with creative and innovative ideas to try and address the questions of processing and building collections, as well as providing or improving services. In approaching how to use volunteers, it helps to identify some needs. Often a need the library has can be matched to a group with an interest and some assistance that can meet that need.

Beginning in 1933 a large wave of emigration saw about 20,000 German-speaking people leave Europe. Forced by persecution or

---

Anne F. Roberts is an expert in bibliographic instruction and was formerly on the staff of the library of the State University of New York at Albany. Address correspondence to her at 13 Norwood Street, Albany, NY 12203.

spurred by political disagreement, they began to leave Germany in 1933 and Austria in 1938.

Organizations and individuals assisted the exiles in securing positions at American universities. Forty-nine refugee scholars were appointed to the faculty of the New School for Social Research in New York. This "University in Exile" became the School's Graduate Faculty of Political Science.

The papers of members of the "University in Exile," focusing on the humanities and the social sciences, form the core of the German Exile Collection at Albany. The collections of individual exiles include correspondence, lecture notes, drafts and final versions of publications, documents, photographs, and working files. They are invaluable to students and scholars who are seeking information on the exiles or on the political, social, and cultural conditions of the period. Some of the donors are still living, and a few of them come each year to use these materials in Special Collections.

Acquisition of materials for the German Exile Collection began in 1976, when John M. Spalek, Professor of German, met many of the exiles and their families while compiling his Guide to the Archival Materials of the German-Speaking Emigration to the United States after 1933. While some emigres had already placed their materials in libraries, others were at that time making decisions about the deposition of their correspondence, manuscripts, and private libraries. Professor Spalek worked with the University Libraries in acquiring the materials, and also tried to help in applying for grants to process the materials. The University Libraries' efforts to get funding for processing were not successful. The collection was not processed, except for a few parts as the librarians in Special Collections found time to work on the papers.

I returned from my sabbatical year with a part-time assignment in Special Collections; I was to highlight and publicize the collections and to get more faculty and students to use them. Since the emigre collection was so interesting, I focused on that. The history department happened to have several foreign students from Germany working on master's degrees in history. I publicized the emigre collection by speaking individually with faculty members whose area of expertise and research was modern European history, encouraging them to explore the collection and direct students to it for research papers.

I felt it would be a good idea to solicit volunteers at a meeting at my home. A group of interested emigres was a fascinating gathering of people to meet. All of them had to begin new careers when they arrived in America; not all of them were Jews; and many of them had subject expertise of interest in individual emigres whose papers we have in the collection. Most of these people were professionals in Europe and were not always able to practice in America.

The Friends of the Libraries volunteers related how much they enjoyed volunteer work in libraries; and the head of Special Collections and the archivist introduced the collection and explained what the volunteers would be doing. They distributed lists of names of emigres whose papers we have, and some volunteers selected the ones they were interested in working on. At that time appointments and parking arrangements were made for the volunteers so that follow up would be assured.

The initial interest meeting was a catalyst. Three committed volunteers now come weekly to work on the emigre collection under the supervision of the head of Special Collections and the archivist. The volunteers were given explicit instructions and directions for working on the materials, and they also had an overview presentation with a tour of the physical space so they could see how their work fit into the overall plan for Special Collections.

These volunteers, along with the graduate student, have provided expertise and time to process collections that would not otherwise have been possible. Because of the interest shown by the community members, the University Art Gallery and Friends of the Libraries applied for, and were awarded, a small grant to show an exhibition of drawings by one of the emigres, Benedikt Dolbin. There are plans to complement this exhibition with a concert of music by emigre composers, "Music in Exile," to attract people from both the university and community to attend.

Academic libraries can use volunteers profitably in ways that will enhance their services. Volunteers can be solicited from a variety of groups: graduate students and targeted members of the community.

IV. POINTS OF DEBATE

Male Reference Librarians and the Gender Factor

Ronald Beaudrie
Robert Grunfeld

In the past, the characteristic stereotypical view of male reference librarians was one of weak and non-masculine individuals. We tend to believe that the present male population in professional librarianship is one that differs from that archetypical concept that was held for so many years. This view of the male librarian is not a realistic outlook on the role of today's male in the field of librarianship, a role which has undergone considerable change over the years.

> The librarian not in an administrative position is expected to be subdued, quiet, respectful, helpful, sensitive, etc. Clearly, one may anticipate that individuals with a forceful, outgoing, overtly expressive personality, those who are active, striving,

---

Ronald Beaudrie is Reference Librarian at the Plainview-Old Bethpage Public Library, Plainview, NY and Adjunct Assistant Professor in the Reference Department of the Hofstra University Library, Hempstead, NY. Robert Grunfeld is District Library-Media Specialist for the Smithtown Public Schools in Smithtown, NY and Reference Librarian at the Plainview-Old Bethpage Public Library, Plainview, NY.

and masterful . . . would not be maximally adapted to the requirements of this occupational role.[1]

We can see the portrayal of male reference librarians in motion pictures as being non-existing entities. In most of the major film works, the role of a librarian has been traditionally, if not overwhelmingly, written for a woman. When one thinks of these roles in 20th century American cinema, two of the classic films that come to mind are *Its a Wonderful Life* starring Jimmy Stewart with Donna Reed and *The Music Man* starring Robert Preston and Shirley Jones. In both instances, the librarians portrayed were women, not men, and their occupations had very little or no significance in the plots of the films.

One of the most beneficial outcomes of the "women's liberation movement" of the 1960-70's period was the actual improvement and growth of women's positions and salaries in the labor force in areas which were previously male-dominated.

Perhaps librarianship, due to its disproportionate gender status, where in some specific fields of librarianship, the ratio of male/female librarians, as indicated in a recent compilation by Carol Learmont and Stephen Van Houten entitled "Placements and Salaries 1987: The Upswing Continues" from the October 15, 1988 issue of *Library Journal*, stands as high as 10:1. This is indeed the case in the specialization of school librarianship.

Our field is one where the importance and contributions of the male minority should be closely reassessed for their value and input. By virtue of the natural attention that is paid to the female majority, the role of the male in today's profession has been largely overlooked. These factors perhaps can explain why, in our opinion, the identity of the male librarian has not been altered to reflect the archetypical concept which has been held by so many for so long.

A recent search of journal articles in various library, humanities, psychological and sociological databases has thus far not shown this field to be, in our opinion, adequately explored.

We hope that this raises an outlook which does not offend, but challenges both men and women alike to view the role of the modern day male reference librarian (public, academic, school, special) in a different, more contemporary and realistic light. Let this serve as an open invitation to others to share their own unique insights into males in the profession of library science.

REFERENCE

1. Wilson, Pauline. *Stereotype and Status*; Librarians in the United States. Weston, Conn.: Greenwood Press, 1982, p. 7.

For Product Safety Concerns and Information please contact our EU
representative GPSR@taylorandfrancis.com
Taylor & Francis Verlag GmbH, Kaufingerstraße 24, 80331 München, Germany

www.ingramcontent.com/pod-product-compliance
Lightning Source LLC
Chambersburg PA
CBHW070724020526
44116CB00031B/1599